Association for the Furtherance of Christianity

Letters and Papers concerning the Coptic Church

In Relation to the Church of England

Association for the Furtherance of Christianity

Letters and Papers concerning the Coptic Church
In Relation to the Church of England

ISBN/EAN: 9783337131074

Printed in Europe, USA, Canada, Australia, Japan

Cover: Foto ©ninafisch / pixelio.de

More available books at **www.hansebooks.com**

ASSOCIATION

FOR THE FURTHERANCE OF

CHRISTIANITY IN EGYPT.

LETTERS AND PAPERS

Concerning the Coptic Church, in relation to the Church of England, under the Primacy of ARCHBISHOP HOWLEY,

1836—1848.

PRINTED FOR THE USE OF THE COMMITTEE.

LONDON, 1883.

PREFATORY.

THE letters printed in the following pages have been preserved among the papers of Archbishop Howley, committed, on his death, by his widow and executrix to the care of his domestic chaplain, on whom he had conferred the Archdeaconry of Maidstone. The papers were gone over and endorsed some years ago, and arranged in their order. Circumstances having recently occasioned a reference to them, in connection with the movement now on foot for the furtherance of Christianity in Egypt, the Archdeacon thought it well, as Chairman of the Committee, to place some of the principal letters and papers in the hands of Mr. Few, and of Mr. Blakiston, the Honorary Secretary of the Association, and other members of the Committee to whom they might wish to show them. Mr. Few and Mr. Blakiston thought fit to call the attention of the Committee to these documents which had been thus communicated to them; and the Committee, at their meeting held on Friday, July 27, requested the Archdeacon to print such portions of the correspondence as he might think desirable, with a brief explanatory statement.

The Committee being engaged in maturing arrangements for making full inquiry, on the spot, as to the steps most expedient to take at the present time for the benefit of the Coptic Church, it appeared that much information, such as was desired, would be found supplied by these records of careful inquiries made, at the period to which they refer, and active steps taken at that time "in full and free consultation with the spiritual Heads of the Coptic Church," for raising it from its present condition. It will be seen that much anxious attention was given, and Christian sympathy shown, in communications carried on, at one time almost from day to day, respecting the state of the Coptic Church,—its deep depression and peculiar difficulties and trials, its constitution and order, its ancient ritual and customs; in regard to the spiritual wants requiring to be relieved, particularly by the publication and circulation among them of the Sacred Scriptures, in the Versions, for which they entertain the highest veneration, of the holy volume to which they make their final appeal;—and, in regard to the arrangements which could be adopted, with the best hope of success, for improved education, specially of those who are designed for the ministry of the Church. There seems a prospect now happily opened, in the providence of God, for turning to full account the inquiries and efforts of past years, which circumstances hindered the carrying on then as was earnestly desired. And the work will manifestly be the more full of hope, if it is in a position to take the character of building on foundations already laid with mutual consent, and resuming the threads, unavoidably dropped, but not broken asunder, of charitable designs entertained, and cordial communication entered into, not only by individuals and religious societies, but by the spiritual heads of the Churches concerned, in the spirit of brotherly love without compromise of catholic truth. It may humbly be hoped that a promise which seems to admit of application, with a special fitness, to a land like Egypt, may be fulfilled to us, " Cast thy bread upon the waters; for thou shalt find it after many days."

B. H.

Precincts, Canterbury,
September 5, 1883.

Rev. H. Tattam *to the* Archbishop of Canterbury.

Bedford, *May* 28, 1836.

My Lord,

I take the liberty to address a letter to your Grace, respectfully to ask, if there are any Coptic or Sahidic manuscripts of the Scriptures in the library at Lambeth. A clergyman in the diocese of Canterbury has suggested to me the probability of such manuscripts being found in your Grace's library.

I some time ago presented the Twelve Minor Prophets in Coptic to the Delegates of the press at Oxford, from the manuscript of Dr. Lee, collated with the manuscript in the Delegates' library, with a Latin translation, and am daily expecting the last proof sheet of them.

I am very anxious that the whole of the Coptic and Sahidic versions of the Scriptures should be published, for the benefit of the biblical student, and shall be most happy to continue my labours, if any more manuscripts can be found.

There are manuscripts in Coptic in the Royal Library at Paris, of the Song of Solomon, and Ezekiel, and Daniel; and Daniel also at St. Germain's. There are manuscripts in the Propaganda at Rome of the four Books of Kings, Job, Isaiah, and Jeremiah in Coptic; and of Isaiah and Jeremiah at Venice; and of Proverbs, Ecclesiastes, and Solomon's Song at Turin; which, with the Pentateuch, and New Testament, published by the University, will nearly comprise the whole of the Scriptures.

Dr. Macbride informs me that the Board of Delegates are unwilling to engage in any expense in collecting materials; but they will be willing to continue the publication of other portions of the Coptic Scriptures.

If it should be in my power to go to France this summer, to copy those manuscripts I have named, I shall be glad to do so. And if I ever should possess the means of going to Italy, for a few months, for the same object, I should most gladly go; but this does not come within the range of human probability. . .

I have unintentionally been led to trespass on your Grace's patience to a greater length than I had contemplated, for which I beg most sincerely to apologise.

I have the honour to be, with great respect,

Your Grace's most obedient humble servant,

HENRY TATTAM,
Rector of St. Cuthbert's.

This letter is marked "A" [Answered.]

REV. H. TATTAM *to the* ARCHBISHOP.

BEDFORD, *June* 4, 1836.

MY LORD,

It is with great reluctance that I presume to address another letter to your Grace; but it has occurred to me that possibly your Grace may be able to point out some source, through which I may obtain copies of those Coptic and Sahidic manuscripts for publication, which are in Italy, which I named in my former letter.

May I take the liberty respectfully to ask if your Grace thinks it probable, that his Majesty's Government would interest themselves to obtain copies of them for that purpose, if an application be made to them?

I would willingly go to Italy myself, and obtain correct copies of all that is valuable there, if it be thought desirable that I should do so, on my necessary expenses being paid; and I should be glad to labour to the utmost, in examining, copying, and obtaining copies of those parts of the Coptic and Sahidic Scriptures which we do not possess.

I should not have thought of asking aid of his Majesty's Government, if I possessed the means of carrying my wishes into effect; but my income is so very limited, that it is with difficulty I shall be able to go to Paris to copy the Song of Solomon, Ezekiel, and Daniel, in Coptic, which are in the Royal Library, where every facility has been promised me.

Trusting your Grace will kindly condescend to pardon this second intrusion on your time and attention,

I have the honour to remain

Your Grace's most obedient humble servant,

HENRY TATTAM,
Rector of St. Cuthbert's.

Letter marked "A" [Answered.]

REV. H. TATTAM *to the* ARCHBISHOP.

DOCTOR'S COMMONS, *June* 13, 1836.
MY LORD,

I had the honour to receive your Grace's letter this morning, as I was leaving home for town, on my way to Paris, to copy the Coptic manuscripts of Solomon's Song, Daniel, and Ezekiel, which are in the Royal Library.

I beg to return your Grace my most respectful and warmest thanks for your kind condescension, and the trouble your Grace has taken respecting the Coptic and Sahidic manuscripts in Italy. I am delighted to find there is a prospect of copies of those manuscripts, which we know do exist, being obtained by the Trustees of the British Museum.

There are four Books of Kings in the Propaganda in Coptic, according to Münter, Alder Biblisch. &c., p. 173, and Job, in Rome (Woide's Fragments, p. 4); Isaiah and Jeremiah in the Propaganda and at Venice (Woide's preface to the Sahidic Fragments); the Song of Solomon, and the book of Sirach in Sahidic, at Turin.

I take the liberty to inclose a letter which I received from Dr. Dujardin of Paris, in March last, who had previously been asked for what sum he would copy Daniel and Ezekiel for me. But as he asked £24, saying they would take him two months to copy in Greek characters, and if they were copied in Coptic characters they would cost a much greater sum, I was obliged at once to decline his services.

I also received a letter from the English Chaplain at Rome, and from the Prussian Envoy, on the subject of the Coptic and Sahidic manuscripts at Rome; which I shall have great pleasure in forwarding to your Grace on my return home, which I hope will be in a month, or at furthest in six weeks.

I most humbly beg your Grace to excuse this very hasty letter, written amidst great interruptions, and I may almost add, confusion.

I have the honour to remain,

With the warmest thanks, and greatest veneration.

Your Grace's most obliged and obedient servant,

HENRY TATTAM.

The letter inclosed, from Dr. Dujardin, is dated Paris, 11th March, 1836, and directed to " Monsieur Henry Tattam, membre de la Société Royale de Londres, care of Messrs. John and Arthur Arch, Booksellers, Cornhill, London." It begins

"Monsieur,

Les très utiles ouvrages que vous avez publiés sur la langue Copte dont je m'occupe depuis fort longtemps, m'ont engagé à soumettre à votre jugement une série d'articles relatifs à la *Grammaire Egyptienne* de M. Champollion le jeune. Je vous adresse aujourd'hui les deux premiers." &c.

Rev. H. Tattam to the Archbishop.

Rue St. Honoré, No. 337, Paris, *June* 22, 1836.

My Lord,

The interest which your Grace has most kindly condescended to take respecting the Coptic manuscripts of the Old Testament, has induced me to trouble your Grace with another letter.

I learned at the Bibliothèque du Roi to-day, that Professor Peyron, the keeper of the manuscripts at Milan, is expected in Paris in the course of a few days; and it has occurred to me, that I may be able to communicate with him respecting the Coptic and Sahidic manuscripts at Milan, and convey to him any proposal the Trustees of the British Museum may think proper to make. Professor Peyron offered some years ago to copy them for me, on certain conditions, which I now forget, but which I then assented to; but he never performed his promise. I suppose he became too deeply engaged in preparing his Coptic Lexicon (which he offered to unite with me in publishing), and which came out just after mine.

I fear I shall be detained here rather longer than I had anticipated; for I had hoped I should obtain access to the manuscripts at four or five o'clock in the morning, and then I and my daughter should quickly copy, and collate them. I however shall improve every moment to the utmost.

I find I have Mr. Burgess' letter with me, which I also take the liberty to inclose to your Grace; it will show the difficulty there is on the spot, of obtaining any information, if the individuals are at all suspected, as he is. I wrote to Professor Maï also respecting the manuscripts last September, but obtained no answer.

I have the honour to remain, &c.,

HENRY TATTAM.

I find on looking for Mr. Burgess' letter that I have mislaid it and cannot find it.

REV. H. TATTAM *to the* ARCHBISHOP.

BEDFORD, *October* 6, 1837.

MY LORD,

I fear your Grace will have some cause to feel that I am frequently troubling your Grace upon a subject in which I confess I feel a deep interest; and the only apology I can now offer to your Grace is the new and unexpected position in which I am now placed.

Mr. Grimshawe called on me a short time since, and asked me to furnish him with the particulars of the Coptic version of the Scriptures, and where the manuscripts are to be found that would complete the publication of it, without naming his object in doing so; I willingly gave him the information required, and in reply I received the inclosed note, which I have taken the liberty to forward to your Grace.

I have told Mr. Grimshawe in reply to his note, that I shall be willing to go to Italy and Egypt, to ascertain what there really is of the Coptic and Sahidic versions, and to obtain copies of all that we do not possess, if the difficulties that now exist are removed; and that I would answer his note more fully at a future period, when I have possessed myself of the information requisite for the purpose.

I should very much prefer to accomplish the objects proposed at my expense, rather than at the expense of any individuals Mr. Grimshawe may think of applying to for that purpose. I have therefore presumed respectfully to ask your Grace if you know of any situation I could fill, that would enable me to do so. Should your Grace know of any one before next spring, I should be most thankful to accept it.

As I am in some measure a stranger to your Grace, I trust I may presume to refer your Grace to *all* who know me, for their opinion of my moral character, and of the way in which I have discharged my ministerial duties. I may also refer to the Bishop of Lincoln, from whom I have received personal kindnesses.

I was eight years gratuitous chaplain to our County Infirmary, until a chaplaincy fund was raised; and during the prevalence of cholera in this town, which was principally confined to my parish, I visited every patient, whether Churchmen or dissenters, and continued my visits until they either recovered or died. I mention these things to your Grace, as they will prove that I have not neglected my duties for literary pursuits (which indeed is fully confirmed by my present number of communicants), and also as a guarantee that I should devote the whole of my time to the objects of my research.

I am sorry to say that I have not quite finished the translation of Daniel and Ezekiel, my numerous engagements having left me but comparatively little time to devote to them.

Hoping that your Grace will kindly condescend to pardon the liberty I have now taken,

I have the honour to remain, &c.,

HENRY TATTAM.

[Upon this letter the Archbishop has made a memorandum, "A. Will speak to Bishop of London—Written since."]

REV. HENRY TATTAM *to* ARCHBISHOP HOWLEY.

BEDFORD, *November* 6, 1837

MY LORD,

I beg to return your Grace my most sincere thanks for your kindness, and for the trouble your Grace has condescended to take respecting the Manuscripts of the Coptic Scriptures.

The language now spoken in Egypt is Arabic; but the Coptic language is used by the Coptic Christians in their religious services continually. A few years ago it was said there were five hundred thousand Coptic Christians in Egypt; but Mr. Lane, in his recent publications on modern Egypt, estimates them at one hundred and fifty thousand.

The Bible Society some years ago published the four Gospels in Arabic and Coptic, in parallel columns, for their use, which I edited for them; the Arabic of which also passed under the correction of Professor Lee. In this way they had their own ancient and received version, with the Arabic, the vernacular language, by its side; and would be able at once to compare them. And I may observe it is in this way that many of their *manuscripts* are written. The Bible Society, I believe, has no intention to print any more of the Coptic Scriptures, but hopes to circulate the Arabic Scriptures among the Copts.

I had a letter from the Coptic Patriarch a short time since, written the 22nd of August last, to acknowledge the receipt of the twelve Minor Prophets, with which he was pleased; and he sent in return the manuscript of Revelation, for Dr. Lee, who sent the book. I have tried to get through him the manuscripts we want; but there appears no prospect of success, although he would give, I am told, every facility to a person who wished to inspect and copy them. Dr. Lee has his letter, which is in Arabic, or I would forward it with its translation to your Grace.

I should be most happy to forward the objects of the Translation Committee of our venerable Society in any way I could, but I doubt whether it can be done in this instance; for I am as anxious to obtain a copy of the Sahidic Scriptures from upper Egypt, as of the Coptic Scriptures from lower Egypt; every fragment of the former being of as great importance to the biblical scholar as the latter, and perhaps more so. But how could I employ any portion of my time about the Sahidic Scriptures, if engaged by the Translation Committee on the subject of the Coptic? If I could embrace both subjects, I should be happy.

There is nearly the whole of the Sahidic Scriptures among the numerous Sahidic manuscripts of the late Cardinal Borgia, at Veletri, near Rome. As it is a private collection, it is questionable whether any one would be permitted to copy those parts of the manuscripts.

I think of writing to Professor Macbride to-morrow, to ask him if he can point out any way in which I can accomplish the object of my wishes; but I fear there is little prospect of his being able to point out any situation that would enable me to do it.

May I further presume to trouble your Grace with a letter I received from Mr. Wilkinson on the subject of Egypt? He resided there twelve years, and has published several works on Egypt.

I have the honour to remain,
Your Grace's most obedient and obliged
humble servant,
HENRY TATTAM.

His Grace the Archbishop of Canterbury, &c.

In the following year (1838) a "Memorial" was drawn up by Mr. Tattam, which is here printed from the MS. preserved among Archbishop Howley's papers, omitting only what is unessential now:

MEMORIAL.

As the Coptic and Sahidic versions of the Scriptures are supposed to have been made about the second century, and are considered of greater authority than any of the oriental versions, and of very great importance to the biblical student, and that no future Polyglot Bible ought to be published without them, several learned friends proposed to me, that, as I had published an Egyptian Grammar and Lexicon, and the twelve Minor Prophets in Coptic and Latin, I should go out to Egypt, Syria, and Italy, and collect all the fragments of these versions that could be found, and afterwards publish them.

That it was equally desirable for the success of Hieroglyphic Literature, that my Egyptian Lexicon should be rendered as complete as possible; and as I had already exhausted all the stores which England and France possessed, this could only be done by going to the East, and examining all the Coptic and Arabic Lexicons, and collecting all the new words found in the manuscripts which I might copy or obtain. They therefore suggested that this should also form part of my object.

They further stated that, as a considerable and continued expense would be incurred in collecting and publishing the manuscripts, an application should be made to Government for a literary pension, to enable me to prosecute these objects.

I at once consented to undertake the task, knowing that the work would be of equal importance to the Coptic Church as to us, as they would obtain correct copies of their own Scriptures. The accompanying testimonials were laid before Her Majesty's Government, which granted £300 towards the expense of my journey with a promise of preferment on my return.

On my arrival in Egypt, in October, 1838, I found that Dr. Dujardin, who had been sent out by the French Government for the same object, had died in Cairo about two months previously, just as he was commencing his labours. In the course of my researches I visited all the convents in Upper Egypt and in and about Cairo, and all the principal ones in Lower Egypt and in the Deserts, and also the Patriarch's Library. I copied and obtained copies of all the portions of the Egyptian versions to be found in the country, and of all the Lexicons.

I also examined the libraries of Italy, and at Naples and Rome discovered some valuable manuscripts, but which I could not copy, as the libraries were then regularly closed for the summer. These have not yet been copied.

I leave Professor Lee, an article in the *Edinburgh Review* for October last, and my Coptic and Sahidic Catalogue, to bear testimony as to whether I have not accomplished the objects of my mission. In addition to the Egyptian manuscripts, I have made the most valuable collection of Syriac manuscripts to be found in Europe, of the greatest age and interest. Among them is a lost work of Eusebius, and two other manuscripts of the most precious kind. They were valued at from one thousand eight hundred to two thousand pounds, if put up to public competition. But I declined to accede to this proposal, as it was said the Emperor of Russia, the King of Prussia, and the French Government would become purchasers, and the most important of the manuscripts would be taken out of the country. I was also unwilling it should ever be said that I had made a market of them. I therefore proposed to His Grace the Archbishop of Canterbury to offer them to the Trustees of the British Museum for the sum I gave for them, viz. £250; trusting that I should receive from Government such preferment as my services in the cause of literature had merited. But the Trustees thought this too great a sacrifice for me to make, being a clergyman with a small income, and at length gave me £750 for them. There are about 300 MSS. of the same kind and age, beautifully written on vellum in the same Desert Convent. These I should have returned and made every effort to secure to this country, and with very little doubt of success, if I had met with that encouragement which I was led to expect. . . .

I gave my Egyptian Lexicon and the twelve Minor Prophets to the Delegates of the Press at Oxford, who published them; and what I am now preparing for the press will go to the public through the same channel.

As my services and labours have been of a national description, I am induced to bring them under the notice of her Majesty's present Government, in the firm hope that I shall receive from Sir Robert Peel, the patron of literature and of the arts, such preferment as he may consider me deserving of.

I venture respectfully to refer to the Bishop of Lincoln, who has long known me, both for my character as a clergyman and my attainments as a scholar. His Grace the Archbishop of Canterbury, who, I believe, has seen most of the documents to which I have referred, would, I have no doubt, if applied to, confirm the truth of my statements. He most kindly said, when I applied for the living of Stapleford Abbotts, that if the Lord Chancellor applied to him, he would with pleasure bear testimony to my merits. But I had no opportunity of availing myself of his condescension.

I have the honour to be

Your most obedient, humble Servant,

HENRY TATTAM.

The grant named in this Memorial having been obtained from the Government in promotion of the object in view, the following Appeal was put forward for subscriptions in aid, to be received by the Rev. T. J. Grimshawe, Biddenham, near Bedford, who took the lead in the matter; Dr. Lee, College, Doctors' Commons; Professor Lee, Cambridge; and others:—

"The Rev. Henry Tattam, A.M. Rector of St. Cuthbert's, Bedford, has long been engaged in preparing for publication, an Edition of the Coptic Version of the Holy Scriptures; and finding it necessary, for the completion of his work, to examine and collate all the accessible manuscripts in the monasteries of Egypt, and in the libraries of Italy, has determined to visit those countries. Her Majesty's Government has been pleased to further his object by a grant of Three Hundred Pounds; but as his unavoidable expenditure cannot be calculated at less than double that sum, his friends have resolved to solicit the aid of those who may be inclined to promote his objects. They have obtained the testimony of several distinguished Coptic scholars as to Mr. Tattam's qualifications for the due performance of the task he has undertaken, and therefore trust that they will not appeal in vain for assistance to those who take an interest in an object no less likely to improve our acquaintance with the ancient language of Egypt, than to become instrumental in reviving scriptural knowledge and piety among the Copts, to whose forefathers, almost in the apostolic age, the Christian Church was indebted of the first versions of the Scriptures."

The subscription list was headed with the Government grant £300, and donations from the Archbishop of Canterbury £10 10s., the Bishop of Lincoln £5 5s., the Bishop of London £5 5s., the Duke of Bedford, the Marquis of Tavistock, Granville Penn, Esq., Dr. Lee, Hartwell, and A Lady, £5 5s. each; the Rev. T. S. Grimshawe, Bedford, £10 10s.; Professor Lee, Cambridge, Francis Pym, Esq. Bedford, and Dr. Macbride, Principal of Magdalene Hall, Oxford, £5 each; Rev. James Donne, Bedford, £2; Dr. Bosworth, Rotterdam, and Rev. G. C. Renouard, Swanscombe, £1 1s. each; Sir William Long, Bedford, £1, &c.

The testimonials referred to by Mr. Tattam as having been laid before the Government included letters addressed to

Mr. Grimshawe by Professor Lee (Bristol, Feb. 19, 1838), Professor Macbride, Oxford; W. Tennant, Esq. Professor of Oriental Languages at St. Mary's College, St. Andrew's; Dr. Leemans, First Conservator of the Museum of Antiquities at Leyden; Dr. Bosworth, Rotterdam; J. G. Wilkinson, Esq., Professor H. H. Wilson, Dr. R. Richardson, Rev. R. Cattermole, Rev. Dr. Nolan, Sir Richard Phillips, Dr. Lee of Hartwell, and others. There were appended two letters from the Bishop of Lincoln, who was at that time Mr. Tattam's Diocesan, and from the Archbishop of Canterbury. These letters were as follows:—

THE BISHOP OF LINCOLN *to the* REV. T. S. GRIMSHAWE.

REVEREND SIR,

I do not feel myself competent to express an opinion respecting the extent of Mr. Tattam's acquaintance with Coptic literature; but I know him to be a learned man, and an exemplary, zealous, efficient parochial minister. It is, indeed, scarcely possible to speak too highly of him in the latter character. If he is enabled to carry into effect his wish to travel into Italy and Egypt, I have no doubt that the results of his researches will be to bring to light many curious and interesting documents, which will tend to illustrate every part of Ecclesiastical History, but especially that which is connected with the Liturgies of the Eastern Church.

I have the honour to be, &c., &c.,

J. LINCOLN.

The Archbishop to Rev. H. Tattam.

Lambeth, *April* 17, 1838.

Dear Sir,

Not being acquainted with Coptic, I fear that anything I can say will add little to the testimonies which you have received from so many persons of literary distinction, both to the importance of the object for which you are desirous of visiting Egypt, and to the attainments which qualify you to avail yourself, to the utmost, of the valuable materials which will probably be found in that country. But I have pleasure in bearing witness to the opinion which is generally entertained of your peculiar fitness for such a mission, to your great respectability as a clergyman, and to your unwearied diligence as a scholar. Your researches, if successful, will throw great light on a branch of Ecclesiastical History which has not been hitherto so much cultivated as its importance deserves.

With every good wish, and with sincere respect,

I remain, &c.,

W. Cantuar.

Soon after his return from Egypt, Mr. Tattam renewed his communications with the Archbishop.

Rev. H. Tattam to the Archbishop.

Bedford, *September* 27, 1839.

My Lord,

I frequently wished to address a letter to your Grace, while in Egypt, on the state of Christianity among the Coptic Christians; but the hope that I should be spared, and that I should at no distant period return to my native country, and that probably your Grace would condescend to favour me with an interview upon this subject, induced me to relinquish the idea of troubling your Grace with a letter. I took the liberty to call at Lambeth Palace on my way home, but your Grace was then in your diocese.[1]

While I was in Egypt, I saw much of the native Christians in every part of the country; and what I saw has more deeply than ever interested me in their spiritual welfare.

It is true that both priests and people are in a very low and fallen condition as a Christian Church. They have the form of Christianity among them; but of its spiritual nature they appear to have no notion whatever. Still, there are many things of a pleasing character which lead me to believe they will one day arise from the dust, and return to a pure faith, and to a corresponding practice and conduct.

I am delighted to find that the venerable Society for Promoting Christian Knowledge has looked with a pitying eye upon this, and other fallen Eastern Churches; and is performing the part of the good Samaritan, in endeavouring to restore them to spiritual health and strength again, by giving them a pure Arabic version of the Scriptures, and an excellent Liturgy in Arabic.

The knowledge of this will encourage me to make an application to the Society, which I have for some months formed the design of doing, if it should meet with your Grace's concurrence and approbation, to solicit the Society to give the Egyptian Christians a good commentary in Arabic, if it be only in the first instance of one Epistle and Gospel.

The Coptic Christians have no Commentary on the Scriptures, except on a few passages, and there are no sermons in the churches; it was therefore correctly said by one some years ago, who was well acquainted with the Copts, and was capable of forming an opinion, that "above all things they want a short

---

[1] The week preceding.

but concise commentary on the Holy Scriptures; and if we could only give them a commentary on one of the Gospels, we should give them an inestimable treasure."

In my last interview with the Patriarch, who had kindly lent me every assistance in the prosecution of my object, I asked him, if the English, who feel interested in their spiritual welfare as a Christian Church, should furnish them with a commentary on the Scriptures in the Arabic, whether himself and others would examine it with one or two Englishmen before it was printed; and anything that should be found objectionable would be well considered; and, if not of an essential nature, I felt persuaded it would be altered so as to suit their views. I at the same time made the Patriarch distinctly to understand, that I had no authority from any person whatsoever to propose such a work; but I knew that many English Christians feel very much interested in their Christian prosperity, and it is possible they may be induced to assist them in this way. He appeared to receive the proposal with real pleasure, and very readily promised to do as was proposed, should such a work be entered upon.

I obtained, while in the East, two copies of the New Testament in Arabic, which was printed on Mount Lebanon. The translations are said to be very excellent and faithful. I shall have much pleasure in presenting one of these copies to the Translation Committee of the Society for Promoting Christian Knowledge, as soon as they arrive.

I have the honour to remain, &c.,

. HENRY TATTAM.

[Upon this letter the Archbishop has made a note, "A. [Answered] Approve his intended application to the Society."]

Rev. H. Tattam to the Archbishop.

Bedford, *October* 24, 1839.

My Lord,

When I was at Jerusalem in April last, Mr. Young, our consul there, expressed his earnest wish that an English clergyman might be appointed for Jerusalem to represent the English Established Church there, and for the benefit of European Protestants who may visit the Holy City. Mr. Young asked me in what way he should proceed to make his wishes known. I advised him to write to your Grace as the spiritual head of the Anglican Church; and at his request I promised to state to your Grace my own impressions respecting such an appointment.

I received the accompanying letter from Mr. Young while in Egypt; and from its contents I presumed he would address a letter to your Grace upon the subject.

I think the state of things in the East is such that an English clergyman might be sent out to Jerusalem with most favourable prospects of success. We have an English consul now at Jerusalem; and I preached to nineteen persons in his house, who understood English, and who were then resident in the city. In addition to these we may mention the numbers of English, and of others who understand the English language, who every year visit Jerusalem, to whom the English services would be an invaluable blessing.

But we should also bear in mind that every other Christian Church is represented in Jerusalem, where, alas! Christianity is exhibited in its worst form by the priests and the thousands of blind devotees of every form of Christianity, and with the mass of superstition, ignorance, and sin, that is every year collected together in Jerusalem from every part of Christendom; and by the blessing of God he might do much good among them.

An exhibition of pure and spiritual Christianity before the Mahometan population could not fail of having a favourable effect upon them; as they now only see Christianity in its worst and most degrading form, upon which they look with contempt, and which only confirms them in their unbelief and error.

There have been some American missionaries in Jerusalem and Syria, but they have not succeeded in their object; and this failure is solely to be attributed to the circumstance of their not being Episcopalians, which is an insuperable obstacle in the way of doing good among Oriental Christians. They had left Jerusalem when I was there; but I believe they intend to return thither again.

I hope and trust that the Society for the Propagation of the Gospel will consent to meet the wishes of the consul, and will appoint a clergyman for Jerusalem who will fully and efficiently represent the Church of England there; and who will constantly labour, amidst all the apathy, indifference, or opposition he may experience, to diffuse, in the spirit of kindness, the knowledge of true scriptural Christianity among those who may assemble there.

I have the honour to remain, &c.,

HENRY TATTAM.

REV. H. TATTAM *to the* ARCHBISHOP.

BEDFORD, *Oct.* 24, 1839.

MY LORD,

When I had the honour of calling upon your Grace the other day, I accidentally referred to the fact of the Pacha's intention to commit the education of his two sons to the clergyman who shall be appointed to Alexandria.

I have searched for a copy of Hehekyan Bey's letter upon the subject in vain; but when I find it, or can procure a copy,

I shall take the liberty to forward it to your Grace, as I think it alludes to the Pacha's intention to place the clergyman at the head of a literary institution, or college, which the Pacha intends to establish at Alexandria. But if I am mistaken in this particular, I know that Hehekyan Bey, who is the Pacha's Minister of Instruction, has expressed this intention of the Pacha to some friends of mine in Cairo.

In the absence of the letter to which I have alluded, I take leave to copy a part of the Report of the Church Missionary Society for this year, pp. 52, 53.

"Mrs. Lieder has obtained access to the Pacha's family for the purpose of imparting instruction to them. They consist of the eldest daughter of Nazly Hanum, the youngest daughter of Geineb Hanum, the wife of Ibrahim Pacha, the wife of Ibrahim Pacha the younger, the wife of Tassoan Pacha, the wife of Abbas Pacha, the wife of Ismael Pacha, the wife of Ahmed Pacha. Another incident, scarcely less remarkable, is an intimation from Hehekyan Bey, the Pacha's Minister of Instruction, that the Pacha thought of committing the education of Mahomet Ali Bey, and his little brother, to the clergyman expected at Alexandria to occupy the church built by the English residents at that place."

I have the honour to remain, &c.,

HENRY TATTAM.

REV. H. TATTAM *to the* ARCHBISHOP.

BEDFORD, *November* 12, 1839.

MY LORD,

I was favoured with your Grace's letter on Thursday last, and take the liberty to say that I entirely concur with the just view which your Grace has taken in reference to the appointment of a clergyman to Jerusalem.

I can with the greatest confidence and comfort rely upon your Grace's judgment and zeal, for maturing and proposing any plans for the extension of the kingdom of Christ among the fallen Churches of the East; and I shall be most glad to commit any information to your Grace which I may possess, or any opinion which I may have formed, to be dealt with as your Grace may think proper: at the same time I shall rejoice if I can supply any information that may be in any degree of a useful nature.

Since I last presumed to trouble your Grace with a letter, I have received a communication from the Reverend W. R. Fremantle, brother to Sir Thomas and Sir William Fremantle, who was in Egypt at the time I was, to ask me to unite with him in drawing up a letter to your Grace and the Bishop of London on the present state of religion in the Eastern Churches, and the prospect to the Church of England of usefulness among them. If I understand him rightly, he wishes to see a bishop appointed to Malta for the Mediterranean, and for missionaries to be sent out from the Propagation Society to the Eastern Churches. He also particularly desires that a missionary may be sent to the Druses on Mount Lebanon, who, Mr. Fremantle says, since Ibrahim Pacha has taken away their books, have generally wished to be instructed in the religion of the English. The American missionaries have been among them, but not being Episcopalians they have not effected much; and the consequence is the Church of Rome is gaining them by scores as converts to her communion. This I learn from Mr. Fremantle, with whom I have declined to unite in his object, although I should be delighted to see a bishop appointed to Malta, and the mission to the whole of the Eastern Churches undertaken by the Society for the Propagation of the Gospel; and I understand this is the view Mr. Bickersteth has also taken of the subject.

As soon as I ascertained that the Church Missionary Society could not increase the number of their missionaries in Egypt for want of funds, I wrote a letter to your Grace respecting the Coptic Christians in Egypt, and also to suggest whether that mission could not be altogether carried on by the Propagation Society, which is much more in connection with the spiritual heads of the English Church, and therefore more likely to be extensively useful.[1] There are now only two missionaries employed in Egypt; and they are almost constantly engaged in the education of children, and but seldom come in contact with the adult population.

The books which were taken from the Druses were given by the Pacha, while I was in Egypt, to Elat Bey, his physician, who is a Frenchman; and he has presented them to the Pope. The duplicates were given to Colonel Campbell, our Consul-General for England.

I forgot to state to your Grace in my former communications, that I have copies of all the liturgies in use in the Coptic Church, which I propose to translate as soon as my numerous engagements will permit me to do so.

I have the honour to remain, &c.,

HENRY TATTAM.

REV. H. TATTAM to the ARCHBISHOP.

BEDFORD, *December* 24, 1839.

MY LORD,

I yesterday received the accompanying letter from the Hehekyan Bey to Mr. Lieder.

I wrote to Miss Hope some time since to ask her to favour me with a copy of the letter; and she has had the kindness to send me the original, which I shall be glad to receive, and

---

[1] [This was prior to the arrangements made by the Society, in regard to its constitution in relation to the episcopate, in 1841.]

return to Miss Hope again at your Grace's leisure, and when it is quite done with. I take the liberty to trouble your Grace with the letter; as it will show the importance of the office the clergyman who may be appointed for Alexandria may have to fill, and the consequent necessity of care in the selection of the individual.

I received a letter from the secretary of the Christian Knowledge Society a few days ago, informing me that there are portions of Ephraim Syrus and of Chrysostom in the commentary translated into Arabic; and he is instructed to ask, if some of those will not answer the end which I have in view, and be more acceptable to the Oriental Christians than any commentary which they could prepare. I am inclined to think the Translation Committee cannot do better than make a careful selection from the Arabic translation of these authors; as anything coming stamped with the authority of these names will be more readily received, and bowed to, by the Oriental Christians, than any modern production, however excellent. My opinion is not of much value; but such as it is, I shall have much pleasure in communicating it in the course of a few days.

I have received a copy of Mr. Fremantle's letter, marked private, and find from the perusal of it, that he has not followed out his original intention in every particular; but I still hope it will have the effect of directing attention to the Eastern Churches, and that an effort will be made to raise them from their present state of ignorance and error.

The state of the Coptic Christians in Egypt has deeply interested me; and I exceedingly rejoice that the Christian Knowledge Society will undertake a work that must be attended with important benefits to them, and other Eastern Christians; and I hope the time is not far distant, when a more extended effort to do them good will be entered upon, and, under the blessing of God, be crowned with important results.

Trusting that your Grace will condescend to pardon the liberty I have taken in giving expression to my feelings and opinions,

I have the honour to remain, &c.,
HENRY TATTAM.

REV. H. TATTAM *to the* ARCHBISHOP.

BEDFORD, *March* 6, 1840.

MY LORD,

My attention has been called to a statement in the *Record* newspaper of March 26th. I have in consequence procured the paper, and read the article with pleasure. As I know your Grace is very much interested in all that is likely to terminate in the spiritual improvement of Egypt, I take the liberty respectfully to inclose it to your Grace.

I have the honour to remain, &c.,
HENRY TATTAM.

REV. H. TATTAM *to the* ARCHBISHOP.

BEDFORD, *March* 6, 1840.

MY LORD,

I had no idea that I should cause your Grace the trouble of replying to Mr. Grimshawe's letter when I took the liberty to inclose it for your Grace's perusal, or I should have taken care to prevent that tax upon your Grace's time. . .

I exceedingly rejoice in the disposition to a friendly intercourse with the Church of England which the Coptic Patriarch has shown; and I most sincerely trust that it will tend, under the blessing of God, to the furtherance of real religion in the Egyptian Church; but I most earnestly hope that no part of the Patriarch's plan to raise his Church is to send young men on to this country to be educated for the ministry. It is so objectionable in every point of view that I most sincerely hope it never will be proposed, and, if it be, that it will never be carried into effect. The end may be more effectually obtained by a Missionary Institution in Egypt, under the *inspection* of the Patriarch and the Bishops, and of a similar nature to the one now in existence at Cairo, but differently conducted. It might be carried on at a much less expense than the education of young men sent to England would cost, and with a much better prospect of success.

I had no doubt, while in Egypt, of the friendly feelings of the Copts towards the Church of England; but I was unprepared for this exhibition of it by the Patriarch.

I drew up a statement last November of the present state of religion in Egypt, and the prospect of usefulness among the Copts, which I intended to forward to your Grace; but as Mr. Fremantle was at that time preparing a letter on the state of the Oriental Churches, I did not then trouble your Grace with it; but as I expect to be in town next week, I will leave it at your Grace's palace. . . .

I am very thankful that the Christian Knowledge Society has decided on printing an Arabic Commentary on the Scriptures from the Arabic translations of the Fathers, the most acceptable work we can present to the Oriental Christians; and the next best work for the Copts would be an edition of the Arabic Homilies of Macarius, which is a very excellent work: I expect an Arabic copy of them shortly from Egypt.

I have translated about half of one volume of Coptic prayers, and am gratified to state that very little of an objectionable nature has yet been met with.

I have lately ascertained that the second son of the Pacha

of Egypt (now living) was partly educated under an Englishman at Alexandria, but whose name I now forget: and I know that the Pacha prefers the English in his service to men of any other country. . . .

I have the honour to remain, &c.,

HENRY TATTAM.

REV. H. TATTAM *to the* ARCHBISHOP.

LONDON, *March* 11, 1840.

MY LORD,

I very much regret to say that I have not been able to bring the letter with me to town, which I wrote on the present state of the Coptic Church, having lost the key of my writing desk where it is deposited.

I will on my return home have the lock broken, and forward the letter to your Grace.

I have the honour to remain, &c.,

HENRY TATTAM.

REV. H. TATTAM *to the* ARCHBISHOP.

BEDFORD, *March* 27, 1840.

MY LORD,

I am afraid of being troublesome to your Grace, and of occupying more of your valuable time than my humble station would justify; and yet I know not how so well to make the information available which I have collected respecting the present state of Christianity in Egypt as by communicating it to your Grace.

It is allowed on all hands that Christianity was established in Egypt at a very early period, and, the Copts say, by St. Mark, who, according to their received traditions, was the first Bishop of Alexandria. However this may be, we know from undoubted authority that no country ever exhibited greater piety, or more sincere and real devotedness to God, than Egypt did for the first three centuries. But, alas! the gold soon became dim, and the fine gold was quickly changed: for the simplicity of the Gospel was soon corrupted by metaphysical subtleties; and heresy, and bitterness, and disgraceful contests speedily followed, and destroyed both the spirituality and vitality of religion. From this period their glory and prosperity as a Christian Church began to decline, until Mohammedanism spread itself over the land; and so they have continued to the present time, with a few variations.

The Coptic Church, which acknowledges the Patriarch of Alexandria as its spiritual head, is called Jacobite, and holds the Monophysite doctrine, or heresy.

The Patriarch of Alexandria generally resides in the Patriarchate at Cairo. He is elected to his office by the Bishops, and clergy, and chief persons among the Christians of Alexandria and Cairo; the election confirmed by the suffrages of the people, and perfected by the consecration of the Bishops. The conditions required are that he shall be thirty years of age, and a Presbyter; that he should be free, and not in captivity, and should possess health and soundness of body, and that he hath never shed blood, or been married; that he should understand and speak the language of the people without an interpreter, and should be able to read and interpret the Coptic books;—he must have a good testimony, even from those who are without; not be soon angry, nor given to drink; not a striker, not greedy of filthy lucre; powerful to labour, that he may be able by word and doctrine to convince the adversaries of the faith; —that he should be orthodox, and not seek the office of Patriarch by the favour of princes or of seculars.

The same conditions apply to the offices of bishop, priest, and deacon, with a slight variation. For instance, a bishop may have been married before he is made a bishop, but he must have been the husband of one wife: and the priests are allowed to marry, but not more than once.

The Patriarch and Bishops have an annual income, which is partly derived from the people, every one of whom is obliged to contribute a small fixed annual sum to the ecclesiastical revenues, and partly from other sources.

The common priests live upon the charity of the people; but they are uneducated men, taken from among the people, and sometimes against their wills forced into the ministry; and consequently, while this system continues, the Copts must, of necessity, have an ignorant and an inefficient ministry.

Besides the Patriarch, who generally resides at the Patriarchate in Cairo, and who is also the head of the Coptic and Abyssinian Churches, the Copts have nine Bishops in Upper Egypt, and three in Lower Egypt; one or more of whom, with the Bishop of Jerusalem, reside with the Patriarch, to assist him in ecclesiastical affairs: the other Bishops reside in their respective dioceses, and visit their churches and congregations from time to time.

To each of their churches there is, generally, attached a school where the children are simply taught to read and write, which is the whole of the prevailing education among the Copts, who are thus prepared to fill the office of clerks under Government; which they do in every part of the country. I found blind Areefs, or schoolmasters, in several of their schools; and this I am told is no uncommon thing.

All causes among the Copts, whether of an ecclesiastical or a secular nature, are decided at the Patriarchate: it is, therefore, absolutely necessary that those whom the Patriarch selects to assist him should understand the canonical laws, and also the common laws or regulations of the country.

The Copts practise circumcision, but not as a religious ceremony; it being a custom, as they say, derived from the Ishmaelites: but they hold it as an indifferent thing, and some of them are circumcised and some not.

The children of the Copts do not receive their names at baptism, but on the seventh day after their birth, as they are usually not baptised until they are six months old. But they never baptise boys until forty days after their birth, nor girls until eighty days; except in cases of the most urgent necessity. They immerse the infants three times in the Name of each of the Persons in the blessed Trinity; and they have sponsors who have the spiritual care of the infants, to teach them the mysteries of the Christian religion until they arrive at the age of fourteen years.

The sacramental bread (which is made in little stamped cakes) is generally administered every Sunday in the Coptic churches, one cake being given to every one who desires it; but the wine is administered to those only who are considered worthy, and then only with a spoon, two or three spoonfuls being given to each communicant.

The Copts have a great reverence for the sacred Scriptures, and appear to bow to whatever is proved from them; and they also consider that every one has a just right to that holy Volume as his guide and directory in the way of life. Although they find fault with the Arabic version of the Scriptures published by the Bible Society, and also with that published by the Propaganda at Rome, yet they do not refuse to receive and use them; on the contrary, they are most eager for copies of the sacred Scriptures in every part of Egypt. But when they shall begin earnestly to inquire what is truth, and return to the simplicity and purity of the Gospel of Christ, their own Coptic version, I have no doubt, will be the standard to which they will appeal; and it is this conviction which has principally influenced me in the wish to obtain a correct text of their own acknowledged version of the sacred Scriptures. We know too little at the present time of the Old Testament in Coptic to be able to pronounce upon it with accuracy; but the Coptic New Testament is a very close translation from the original Greek.

It is true that "the Church of Alexandria," as our Nineteenth Article expresses it, "has erred"; and it is still in error, as well as in deep ignorance and moral degradation; but there are many circumstances which induce me to believe, that that Church may be raised from its present position and be brought back to apostolical purity: and most certainly they have never been in so favourable a state for the effort to be made as at the present time. Now all religions are equally tolerated and protected in Egypt; and all persons are appointed to offices of trust in the Government without any reference to their religious creed.

Another singular feature in the present state of Egypt is not only the diminution of Mohammedan prejudice in the best instructed part of the population, but the favourable light in which the professors of religion are viewed by the Government. We have a proof of this in the fact that a certificate given to any boy by our missionaries in Egypt, stating that he is receiving instruction in their schools, is a sufficient protection from being seized either for the army or any other Government purpose. I may also mention that the Pacha's second son, now living, was in part educated under the tuition of an Englishman; and the Pacha last year intimated, that he had some intention of committing the education of his two sons to the English clergyman who should be appointed to the chaplaincy at Alexandria. How far the termination of the affair now pending between Turkey and Egypt may affect this intention remains to be seen. I was also repeatedly assured, while in Egypt, that an English missionary who could speak the Turkish language might find ready access to the principal

Turks; and that his statement respecting Christianity would be attentively and respectfully listened to; and of the truth of this statement I myself have no doubt.

If the Coptic Church ever returns to the purity of the Gospel in faith and practice, as I believe it will, it appears evident that the agency most likely to bring about this desirable object is a pure episcopal church; and where is one to be found so nearly answering this character as the Church of England? There are also other circumstances which point out the Church of England as more peculiarly fitted for this great and holy undertaking. The resources which the Church of England possesses are fully equal to all that lies before her; and I have no doubt that the people of this country would respond to any call to enable her to carry out any designs to their fullest extent. The influence, also, of the English name is very great throughout the East; nor is it at all weakened if the individual who bears it be a clergyman.

The Church of Rome is continually alive to every favourable circumstance for the extension of her ecclesiastical dominion in the East, and is always prepared to improve it to the uttermost. Some time since the Pope presented the Pacha of Egypt with a magnificent snuff-box and other valuables, through the French consul; and he has lately had a return made. The Pacha has offered to the Pope four magnificent columns of alabaster, which are intended to adorn the new church of St. Paul at Rome.

I trust the Church of England will not be found less zealous than the Church of Rome in spiritual matters, and in her endeavours to extend the Redeemer's kingdom. May she be steadfast and unmovable, always abounding in the work of the Lord, knowing that her labour will not be in vain in the Lord.

I have the honour to remain, &c.,

HENRY TATTAM.

P.S.—I have not been able to get at the letter which I wrote some months ago on this subject. I have, therefore, written another, which I will not trouble your Grace to acknowledge the receipt of. When I called at Lambeth Palace a fortnight ago, it was simply to deliver the Coptic sacramental bread to your Grace's servant, and not to seek an interview with your Grace, as I had nothing to communicate that would justify me in trespassing upon your Grace's valuable time for a moment. I beg to return your Grace my most sincere thanks for your condescension; but I have nothing to induce me to avail myself of it at the present.

Rev. T. S. Grimshawe *to the* Archbishop.

Jerusalem, *April* 7, 1840.

My Lord Archbishop,

The state of my health having made it necessary that I should spend the winter in a more southern climate, it has been my object to combine with the recovery of my strength such opportunities of usefulness as circumstances and the providence of God might present. From experience I may add that these opportunities are ample; and that, if *Christian travellers* were more numerous in the parts of the world which I have visited, much valuable information might be collected, and openings presented for a more enlarged sphere of zealous and pious exertion than is generally, I think, entertained. I more particularly refer to the Eastern Churches, as having come most under my contemplation, and standing most in need of our assistance. At Alexandria I found the public worship of God on the Sabbath day wholly dependent on the casual presence of ministers, often of different communions; and at the period of my arrival, which was in December last, there had been an entire suspension of services for some weeks. I arrived on the Saturday evening; and, though I lost no time in communicating my readiness to officiate if necessary, I was informed by the vice-consul that the place was too unprepared for the reception of a congregation at so short a notice; but that on the ensuing Sunday it was the intention of Colonel Campbell, the consul-general (then on the eve of relinquishing his office) to lay the first stone of an intended new church; and that he was commissioned to request that I would give to the ceremony a religious and ecclesiastical form and character. I need not assure your Grace with what willingness I profited by this opportunity. We met at the appointed time at the British consulate. A numerous and highly respectable assemblage of European residents, English, Scotch, French, and Dutch, walked in procession, with music and the British standard. Colonel Hodges, the new consul-general, was present; prayers and a suitable address were offered; in the course of which I expressed my sincere hope that the pious enterprise, commenced by one consul, might be brought to its due consummation by his successor. This assurance was given with great cordiality and earnestness by Colonel Hodges; and the sum of money already raised amounts, I understand, to about £700. It is extremely important that a minister be selected for this situation who may command respect by his piety, and general qualifications and manners; and his usefulness and income will be considerably augmented, if he be competent from his classical and other attainments to take pupils.

From Alexandria I continued my tour to Cairo. After much serious deliberation, founded on the existing state of the Coptic Church and the general aspect of things in Egypt, I thought I was not exceeding the limits of duty and responsibility in soliciting the honour of an interview with the Coptic Patriarch, and, as an English clergyman, expressing to him, in the name of my own Church, a Church illustrious for its Apostolical origin, its constitution of bishops, priests, and deacons, its ancient creed and liturgies, its long list of confessors and martyrs, its past tribulations, and its singular preservation by the providence of God till the present day in the midst of severe trials and difficulties. To these expressions of regard the Patriarch was pleased to reply, that he was deeply sensible of these assurances of sympathy and respect on the part of the Church of England, a Church well known to him by name and reputation; that they (the Copts) had long been a suffering Church for the cause of the truth, and were still prepared to suffer, if such were the will of God. I then adverted to the present position of Egypt, the introduction of European art and science, its tendency, unless duly curtailed and regulated, to lead to infidelity, the symptoms of approaching dissolution in the Turkish empire, and the importance of replacing the fall of error by erecting on its ruins the cross of Christ. I took occasion from this to dwell on the duties and high responsibilities of all Christian Churches in times like these—that they were cities set on a hill, that their light was to shine, that the eye of God and of the world was fixed upon them, and that He had authoritatively declared, "all the churches shall know that I am He which trieth the reins and searcheth the heart," that the Coptic Church had now a great duty to perform, that an immense field of usefulness lay before it, and that it might, by the grace of God, become the instrument of great good; but that for this end there must be a corresponding rise and elevation of piety and zeal in its own members, and especially among its clergy, because the character and spirit of the clergy would always determine that of the people; that if, to accomplish these high purposes, efforts were necessary beyond the means and resources of the Coptic Church, whether his Holiness was willing to accept the aid and cooperation of the Church of England, provided that cooperation could be obtained. On this point I assured him that public attention had recently been much drawn to the Coptic Church; that the

Mission of the Rev. Henry Tattam had excited great interest; that I knew his Grace the Archbishop of Canterbury shared deeply in this feeling, and that some other dignitaries of our Church concurred in the same sentiments. I then adverted to the points of resemblance between the two Churches—both were episcopal in their constitution and liturgical in their services; and with respect to creeds, the fact of that of St. Athanasius, one of their own Bishops, being incorporated with our own Services, furnished a strong evidence of the degree of approximation in the higher and more fundamental principles of our holy Religion, however we might differ in some other respects; and that, lastly, each Church recognised the sacred Scriptures as the supreme standard of faith and practice. I concluded, therefore, by stating that these various points of resemblance furnished sufficient ground for an alliance between the two Churches on the principle of mutual independence, but implied aid and cooperation on the part of the Church of England; and that this aid might be extended to the education of the clergy, the establishment of schools, and the distribution of the sacred Scriptures. His Holiness was pleased most fully to express his cordial acquiescence in these propositions; and it was agreed that the details should be laid before him on a subsequent occasion. The Rev. Mr. Lieder, the missionary employed by the Church Missionary Society at Cairo, was accordingly instructed to draw out the plan, comprising these several objects; and on my return from Upper Egypt in the beginning of February last, the document was submitted first of all privately to his Holiness, when it received his approbation with the promise of his signature and patriarchal seal. But on the following day, when the subject underwent a renewed discussion, in the presence of several leading members of the Coptic Church, his Holiness observed, "I give my fullest sanction to the propositions contained in this document, and am willing to see it carried into effect; but so exposed am I to animadversion and remark, in all that I say or do, that I am convinced, if I were to give my signature and patriarchal seal, as suggested, the publicity of the act, under present existing circumstances, would endanger its success, and probably be the most effectual mode of defeating its execution. I trust, therefore, that my word will be deemed sufficient; and yet, whenever I can safely affix my signature and seal, I shall be most willing to afford it."

The rest of the assembly unanimously concurred in the wisdom of this measure; and some of them remarked, "Sir, the word of the Patriarch is the same as his seal and signature." This discussion lasted two hours and a half, during which every proposition underwent the most minute investigation; and one of the persons present to whom the Patriarch seemed particularly to refer, observed, "He who cannot assent to the propositions contained in this document does not deserve the name of a Christian." The interview concluded with general expressions of satisfaction at the prospect of a measure so calculated to strengthen the interests of the Coptic Church, and to infuse new energy into its proceedings. It seems that the object of the meeting had transpired, and excited attention; for on our return the entrance and court were crowded with Copts, who showed us much respect as we passed; but the most gratifying fact that came to our knowledge was the following—that during the last three weeks (one week after our first discussion) three meetings had been established in the Coptic quarter of Cairo, consisting of from thirty to fifty members, for the express purpose of reading the Scriptures every evening in the week, except the eve of the Sabbath. This spirit of inquiry will, I trust, prove the prelude of a revival. It was exciting much attention; and the Rev. Mr. Lieder informed me, that on every side people were exclaiming, "*This is the work of God.*"

I ought to have apprised your Grace, that it was judged highly expedient that the proposed scheme of education for the clergy should be carried into effect *not in England, but in Cairo*, and under the superintendence of the Patriarch. It will obviate many difficulties which I have not now time to enter upon; and the instruments are at hand, fully competent to give it the required efficiency. The Rev. Mr. Lieder and the Rev. Mr. Krusé, both of Basle, the former of whom has been resident at Cairo for thirteen years, are willing to act, if an arrangement could be made with the Church Missionary Society to whose Mission they belong; and the latter has raised up many instruments competent to act as schoolmasters: but I defer these points till I have the honour of paying my respects to your Grace on my return to England towards the middle or end of June.

I am sorry this letter has extended to so great a length; but the nature of its contents must plead my apology.

I have the honour to be, with great respect,

Your Grace's very obedient servant,

T. S. GRIMSHAWE.

The number of the Copts is, I believe, estimated at above 150,000; and the patriarch informed me they had eleven Bishops at that time, and that he was shortly to consecrate one more which would complete the required amount.

[The above letter was "Received June 12, 1840."]

DETAILS OF A PLAN DRAWN UP AT THE REQUEST OF THE REV. T. S. GRIMSHAWE, BY THE REV. THEOPHILUS LIEDER, AGENT OF THE CHURCH MISSIONARY SOCIETY, CAIRO, AND PRESENTED TO HIS HOLINESS THE COPTIC PATRIARCH; AND, AFTER BEING APPROVED AND RATIFED BY HIM, TO BE PRESENTED TO HIS GRACE THE ARCHBISHOP OF CANTERBURY AND TO THE LORD BISHOP OF LONDON.

First,—The establishment of an *Institution for the training of young men for the ministry,* comprising the necessary instruction in everything which may qualify them, by the Divine grace and blessing, to become "the ministers of Christ and stewards of the mysteries of God" (1 Cor. iv. 1).

Rules for the Regulation of the above Institution.

The Institution shall commence with twenty-four pupils, to be selected from the deacons and archdeacons [1] of the twelve churches in Cairo and the surrounding districts, of which every church might send two. Should it, however, be found that any of these are not endowed with the requisite qualifications for the sacred office, others may be chosen and received, as may be judged most expedient, in their stead.

The pupils of the Institution shall be boarders, receiving their food and clothes, if deemed necessary, and shall be entirely under the control of the principal of the establishment; but they shall be permitted to see their friends and relatives at such times as may be appointed. On Sundays and other festivals they shall have permission to attend their duties at their respective churches during Divine service.

The Principal shall be a Minister of the Church of England, to whose care and direction shall be committed the general education of the pupils, and the superintendence of the other teachers; to be appointed with the sanction of his Grace the Archbishop of Canterbury and the Lord Bishop of London, and the concurrence of the Patriarch of the Chair of St. Marcus.

The Patron of the Institution shall be His Holiness the Patriarch, who will form, as may be advisable, a Committee for his aid, which may consist of one Bishop, two Kumuses,[2] three priests, and six respectable and well-educated laymen. It shall

---

[1] The deacons and archdeacons, instead of having arrived at years of maturity, as is the practice with us, are usually youths of fourteen or fifteen years of age.

[2] A title synonymous with that of archdeacon of *maturer years* and *higher authority* than those previously mentioned.

be the object of this Committee to protect and support by their influence the above Institution, and also to superintend its proceedings, by visiting it, collectively or individually, as often as they please; in order to ascertain that nothing is done or taught in it, except what has been fully agreed upon, and thus be enabled to vindicate the conductors of it from all suspicion of perverting it to any interested or party purposes, and thereby extend its efficiency and success.

P.S.—Mr. Lieder estimated the expense of the proposed seminary at about £500 per annum.

I shall be happy to afford any further information to your Grace that may be deemed necessary; and I beg to add that I expect to be in town early next week, and shall be most willing to wait on your Grace any morning most convenient. A line addressed to me at Messrs. Hatchard's, booksellers, Piccadilly, will reach me.

[Endorsed by the Archbishop, "Sat. July 18."]

Course of Instruction.

1. The pupils shall receive instruction during the week *in the Coptic language*, in reading, writing, and grammar; in translating from the Coptic into the Arabic, and from the Arabic into Coptic, so as fully to understand and render themselves proficients in the ancient language.

2. *In the Arabic language*, in reading, writing, grammar, and exercises in composition, until they are able to compose a sermon, according to the prescribed and standard rules.

3. Exercises in declamation, as a preparation for public preaching.

4. In arithmetic, geography, general history, ecclesiastical history, the history of the Old and New Testaments, with their chronology.

5. A considerable portion of time shall be appropriated to

the study and examination of the contents of the sacred volume; for which purpose the writings of the most approved Fathers, and especially those of St. Clemens of Alexandria, Athanasius, Cyril, and Chrysostom, shall be made use of, in as far as the writings of the said Fathers can be acquired, and may be found serviceable to that end.

6. A public examination shall be held every three months, to ascertain the progress of the pupils, at which all that are desirous may attend.

7. Every pupil thus trained shall remain in the Institution until His Holiness the Patriarch shall consider him fit for ordination, and appoint him priest to a church.

8. The printing of extracts and compilations from the most approved works of the Fathers belonging to the Coptic Church, or whose writings are approved by it.

9. A commentary on the New Testament in the vernacular language of the country, as proposed to be executed by the Rev. Henry Tattam.

Secondly,
The establishment of schools, on an enlarged scale, for the education of youth.

Thirdly,
The distribution of the Holy Scriptures, gratuitously where necessary.

These resolutions having been privately submitted to his Holiness the Patriarch for his approbation, he was pleased to express his intention of ratifying them by his signature and patriarchal seal on the day appointed for that purpose.

At an interview held with the Coptic Patriarch this day, February 13th, in the presence of several of the most distinguished members of the Coptic Church, the above document having been taken into serious consideration, his Holiness was pleased to assign many reasons for not affixing to it his patriarchal seal; but he most unequivocally expressed *his cordial adherence to its spirit and purport*, in which declaration he was supported by all the members of his Church then present. He also signified his intention formally to give his name and signature, whenever difficulties of a *political nature*, now existing, are diminished or fully removed.

(Signed)   T. S. GRIMSHAWE,

Rector of Burton, Northamptonshire;
Vicar of Biddenham, Bedfordshire.

CAIRO, *February* 13*th*, 1840.

BIDDENHAM, NEAR BEDFORD,
July 17, 1840.

MY LORD ARCHBISHOP,

I have the honour to transmit to your Grace the details of the plan submitted to the Coptic Patriarch by me at Cairo, February 13th, for his approbation and sanction. The reasons assigned by his Holiness for withholding his signature and patriarchal seal were founded on the apprehension of defeating the measure by giving to it a premature publicity; and he was pleased to confirm this view of the subject by many remarks which showed the expediency and wisdom of such a decision. I entertain no doubt of his sincerity. There was an honesty and frankness in his manner strongly indicative of his friendly feelings and cordial approbation of the object; and a similar spirit pervaded the whole meeting. Should the proposed co-operation be given to the Coptic Church by the Church of England, the mode seems to be as practicable as the results are likely to be beneficial and important—involving the revival of this ancient but now depressed Church, and thus raising up an instrument for diffusing Christianity in Egypt; and extending its benefits in Abyssinia (of which he is also Patriarch), and where, I understand, there are two millions of professing Christians, but without the vital power of godliness. Allow me, my Lord Archbishop, to recommend this cause to your peculiar favour and consideration, and to that of the Lord Bishop of London. May your Primacy be signalised by an act that will embalm your memory in the gratitude of your own Church, and secure for you the prayers and benedictions of an ancient Church, coeval with the times of the Apostles; once valiant for the faith, but now alas! desolate and fallen; and yet still capable, by God's blessing and man's charity, to become "a light shining in a dark place," and "a praise in the earth."

I have the honour to be, with the greatest respect,

My Lord Archbishop,

Your Grace's most obedient and faithful servant,

T. S. GRIMSHAWE.

[These letters and papers bear the marks of having been much used].

REV. H. TATTAM *to the* ARCHBISHOP.

BEDFORD, *June* 22, 1840.

MY LORD,

I took the liberty a short time ago to forward to your Grace a copy of a letter which I had received from Mr. Grimshawe from Smyrna, my daughter having permitted Mrs. Grimshawe to take away the original. My daughter has since then received a letter from Cairo, stating that there are in Cairo, with the sanction of the Patriarch, six daily meetings of the Copts, in different parts of the city, for the purpose of reading the sacred Scriptures; and the greater part of these have existed from the time I was there.

I have also much pleasure in forwarding to your Grace a copy of the catalogue of the Syriac manuscripts which I brought from Egypt, having received the catalogue from Professor Lee a few days ago; and I hope shortly to be able to add to this the catalogue of the Coptic and Sahidic manuscripts which I copied and obtained in Egypt.

I am exceedingly sorry that Professor Lee has made known from whom the Syriac manuscripts were obtained: for there are probably three hundred very old and beautiful Syriac manuscripts on vellum, now remaining in the same dark cave under the tower in the monastery, and nearly a cart-load of loose leaves which will perfect every manuscript. These it is my intention, if I ever possess the means, to make an effort to secure to England; and I have little doubt I should succeed, unless some foreigner should find them out, who would either obtain them, or by his injudiciousness seal them up from the world. I had two journeys of eight days each for those I have obtained; and my servant had two other journeys of the same length. But I have six volumes which have not arrived in England as yet.

I have not been able to proceed with the preparation of the Coptic Scriptures for the press as fast as I had hoped to do, in consequence of a weakness on the chest, brought on some months ago by an excess of duty; and I have lately been impeded by a newspaper controversy with Lord Shrewsbury's priest, in consequence of some violent letters of his which I was reluctantly obliged to answer, as I was informed they were doing much harm.

I hope now to devote my time to the manuscripts which lie before me.

      I have the honour to remain, &c.,

            HENRY TATTAM.

Catalogue of the Rev. H. Tattam's Syriac MSS.

No. 1.—The latter part of the Prophecy of Ezekiel, A.D. 726. Cyril of Alexandria on the Trinity, A.D. 611, *i.e.* 1,229 years old.

* * *

34. Jacobite Ritual for the whole year, A.D. 1034.
35. Ditto, imperfect, with Lessons.
36. Ditto, ditto, ditto.
37. Ditto, ditto, ditto.

* * *

Rev. H. Tattam *to the* Archbishop.

Bedford, *May* 7, 1841.

My Lord,

I have had the honour to receive your Grace's kind communication this morning, for which I beg to return your Grace my most sincere thanks.

I had written a note to your Grace last night, but it was too late for the post, respectfully to say that I have made up my mind to offer my Syriac manuscripts to the Trustees of the British Museum, . . . and the only condition I will venture to propose is, that the sum which I borrowed to purchase them, which is about £200, may be repaid.

I know that, in taking this step, I shall be acting contrary to the advice and wishes of my friends, and I may be a considerable loser in a pecuniary point of view; but I shall stand in a position which I shall always be able to contemplate with pleasure, whatever my friends or my own family may think of it.

I beg to state to your Grace that I have given Professor Lee permission to copy and publish the lost work of Eusebius; for which purpose I hope he will be allowed to retain the manuscript until he has done with it. The other manuscripts I will direct to be sent to the British Museum as soon as I learn that the Trustees consent to receive them.

But should the funds of the Museum not allow of the money I owe on account of the manuscripts being repaid, I shall then feel myself at liberty to offer them to the Curators of the Bodleian for what they may be considered to be worth.

The Coptic manuscripts I have no intention of selling; as I stand pledged to the public to prepare all the portions of the Scriptures for publication, and a new edition of my Egyptian Lexicon; and to these every spare hour is devoted, now I have finished my controversy with Lord Shrewsbury's priest, who I believe will not venture to appear again in print . . .

I have the honour to remain,

With the greatest respect, &c.,

HENRY TATTAM.

REV. H. TATTAM *to the* ARCHBISHOP.

BEDFORD, *May* 13, 1841.

MY LORD,

I beg to return your Grace my most fervent and heartfelt thanks for the letters which your Grace has done me the honour to write to me, and for the interest which you have condescended to take in my behalf.

I have written a formal letter to your Grace on the subject of the manuscripts, and shall be pleased to leave the matter in the hands of the Trustees of the British Museum . . .

I have the honour to remain, &c.,

HENRY TATTAM.

BEDFORD, *May* 13, 1841.

MY LORD,

I beg to thank the Trustees of the British Museum for their kindness, through your Grace, and to say that the whole cost of the manuscripts was such that I could not afford to give that to the British Museum, but beyond that I will leave the matter in the hands of the Trustees to grant me such an additional sum as they may think proper.

I have the honour to remain, my Lord,
Your Grace's most obedient humble servant,

HENRY TATTAM.

Should the Trustees wish to see the manuscript with Professor Lee, it can be sent to the Museum.

REV. H. TATTAM *to the* ARCHBISHOP.

BEDFORD, *May* 17, 1841.

MY LORD,

In answer to the most kind communication of your Grace, and of the Trustees of the British Museum, with the tender of my warmest thanks for the kindness shown to me, I beg to say, as they have allowed me to amend my offer of the manuscripts to the Trustees, that, in addition to the sum which I gave for the Syriac manuscripts, I shall be glad to receive what they may be considered to be justly worth . . .

I have requested the manuscripts to be forwarded to the British Museum, where I presume they will arrive in the course of a few days, and I will post a catalogue to Mr. Forshall to-day or to-morrow. It is the most splendid collection of Syriac manuscripts I ever saw; and I think it will be found to be equal or superior to any other in Europe.

I have the honour to remain, &c..

HENRY TATTAM.

Rev. H. Tattam *to the* Archbishop.

BEDFORD, *May* 19, 1841.

My Lord,

I have to apologise to your Grace for having caused you the trouble to write two or three letters to me on the subject of the Syriac Manuscripts. . . . I am delighted with the certainty of a Bishop being appointed to Malta, which I feel persuaded will be attended with most beneficial results.

I learn from Mr. Lieder, the senior Missionary at Cairo, that he is requested by the Committee of the Church Missionary Society to return to England for Episcopal ordination, and that the Society contemplate carrying out the plan recommended by the Patriarch for spiritually raising their Church. From Mr. Lieder's last letter, I expected him in England before this time; and I think it is probable that he has arrived by the last vessel.

Mr. Lieder informs me, in answer to inquiries, that " The Copts do not possess the Homilies of Macarius in the Arabic language. The Coptic Patriarch was even astonished when I told him that we possessed these in Greek and Latin. The Copts possess, from the writings of the ancient Fathers, nothing more than a few Homilies of St. Athanasius, Mar Ephraim, and the Homilies and Commentary on St. John's Gospel by Chrysostom. All their other works are commentaries, but are only most superficial compilations. I sent lately to Mr. Schlienz two very scarce Arabic Manuscripts, namely, a Commentary on the Four Gospels, with very interesting Prefaces, by Abu Faraj, as also a Commentary on the Psalms, from the first to the eighty-first Psalm, by the same author; very valuable works, but used by the Copts with much suspicion, as the writer of them seems to have been a Nestorian."

I think I shall take the liberty to forward a copy of this part of Mr. Lieder's letter to the Translation Committee of the

Christian Knowledge Society, as it may prove useful to them. I hope to get the Homilies of Macarius translated into Arabic, through Mr. Kruse, the present missionary in Cairo, with as little delay as possible, and shall hope to see them printed, after being carefully revised, as an earnest of our wish to benefit the Coptic Church.

I have the honour to remain, &c.,

HENRY TATTAM.

REV. RUDOLPH THEOPHILUS LIEDER to the ARCHBISHOP.

41, BLACKMAN STREET,
CORNER TRINITY STREET, BOROUGH,
November 26, 1841.

YOUR GRACE

Will no doubt remember that, some time ago, the Rev. Mr. Grimshawe had the pleasure of presenting the minutes of a plan which had been proposed to His Holiness the Coptic Patriarch, as it respects the future educational advancement of the Coptic priesthood. I have now the honour of inclosing to your Grace a letter directly from the hands of the Patriarch, in which he fully expresses his approbation and ready adoption of the said plan.

Should your Grace wish for further information on this momentous subject, and in as far as my past experience (as missionary in Egypt) may enable me to enlarge on any required point, I am ever ready to wait upon your Grace at any appointed time.

I have the honour to remain

Your Grace's,

Most humble and obedient Servant,

RUDOLPH THEOPHILUS LIEDER.

A Literal Translation of the Letter of His Holiness the Coptic Patriarch.

The Seal.

the Salvation. Petrus, the one hundred and ninth Patriarch of the Chair of St. Mark of Alexandria, Cairo, and Abyssinia. In God.

In the name of God the Benevolent the Merciful.
In God the Salvation.

The peace of our Lord, our God, and our Saviour, and Author of our life, Jesus Christ, who descended upon the assembly of the holy disciples in the noble and majestic hall of Sion, and filled their hearts with mysteries and lights, and gave them power to forgive sins, trespasses, and crimes; may the same Divine peace in its source and abundant security be given, in spiritual love and apostolic charity, to the person of our beloved brother, his Grace the Archbishop of Canterbury. May the Lord God preserve him.

After abundant spiritual salutation and exuberant affection to him, may the grace of Christ remain upon him. And if you deign to ask about our lowliness—many thanks to God—we are in good health and strength, through the blessing of your prayers and assistance of our Lord; and we are only inquiring after your perfect health, if it pleases God, we trust you are in laudable conditions.

Moreover it is not concealed from your eminent Holiness that some time ago Mr. Grimshawe, Mr. Lieder, and Mr. Krusé, the English clergymen, residing now in Cairo for many years, called upon us, and informed us that the above-mentioned Mr. Grimshawe wishes to open an Institution for the education of youth that are fit for the dedication to the order of priesthood for the

Coptic Church of St. Mark. At the same time they presented to us a plan for our inspection, that the arrangement of the Institution should be according to the same, and that the Principal of this institution should be a clergyman of the English Church; this we have accepted with entire approbation, because (of?) the English Church being drawn towards our Coptic Church of St. Mark. But if the Institution should not succeed, we are not to be answerable for the expenses, and if it succeeds, we are also not answerable for the same; and upon this basis were made the conditions, consent, and agreement.

And as our son, Mr. Rudolph Theophilus Lieder, the clergyman, is departing, he requested of us this letter to your Holiness for your consideration.

May you always be in good health; and may our Lord preserve your life, and prolong your days for a long time! Amen.

October the 2nd, 1841.

[Translated by Mr. Lieder.]

REV. H. TATTAM *to the* ARCHBISHOP.

BEDFORD, *December* 14, 1841.

MY LORD,

I went to town last week to meet Mr. Lieder from Cairo, who, I find, has been the bearer of a letter from the Coptic Patriarch to your Grace. Mr. Lieder informed me, that, at his last interview with the Patriarch, after he had stated to Mr. Lieder, in reference to the proposed plan for the education of the priesthood, that he could not allow him to attack his Church, he requested Bishop Abraham, the Coptic Bishop of Jerusalem, whom I well remember, to withdraw. He then said to Mr. Lieder, "I know there are some things in our Church which you consider errors, such as the adoration of saints, &c., and the sooner you can do away with them the better; but this can only be done through the medium of education." I have thought this information so important, that I trust your Grace will pardon me for troubling you with it.

I do not now remember the particulars of the proposed plan of education; but I hope every concession will be made, consistent with principle, to convince the Patriarch of the sincerity and integrity of our intentions.

I am glad to hear that I have every prospect of obtaining the whole of the Coptic Scriptures; as Abuna Tecla, a priest at the Patriarchate, has heard of their being in two places in Upper Egypt, and Mr. Lieder has sent him to purchase them, or to get them copied for me; for which I have furnished him with funds.

The Patriarch, I am informed, has expressed an earnest desire for the whole of the Scriptures in Coptic and Arabic, for the use of his people; and Mr. Lieder intends to apply to the Bible Society for the grant, and has requested me to edit the Coptic part of the work, which I have consented to do. But, as my connection with the Bible Society has for some time ceased, I should be glad to advise him to apply to the Christian Knowledge Society in preference, if I knew there was any prospect of success. He has distributed 1100 copies of the Scriptures this year with his own hands.

If the proposed system of education be carried out, the Patriarch wishes to have a Coptic Arabic Lexicon, which he possesses, printed for the use of the students, and which they will not be able to do without.

The Patriarch has also suggested the desirableness of sending a Coptic priest to edit the Arabic part of the Scriptures, as there are considerable errors in the Arabic of those parts which have been published in Arabic and Coptic; and Mr. Lieder says this might be done at comparatively little expense, and the same person might superintend the printing of the

Arabic part of the Lexicon. I have encouraged the idea, as it probably would give confidence to the Patriarch, and might, under the blessing of God, terminate in the spiritual good of the individual. If one should come, I would gladly take charge of him—find him economical accommodation near me—receive him into my own study, and watch over him with the greatest care—teach him English, and direct his studies in reference to his future usefulness in the Coptic Church. I would guarantee the perfect integrity of the Coptic text of the Scriptures, and take care that no alterations would be made in the Arabic without submitting it to any appointed tribunal. Indeed, I should be glad to take care of two Copts to educate for the Ministry in their own Church; and all I do will be gratuitously done.

I am exceedingly sorry to hear from Mr. Lieder that the most learned in Egypt, both Sheiks and Christians, cannot understand the Arabic used in the new translation of the Scriptures now being printed in Malta; and he says he has ascertained that it is equally unintelligible to the learned in Syria.

Your Grace's kindness and condescension have permitted you to speak of my daughter's, or rather step-daughter's *Journal* in such terms as she feels to be a rich reward for permitting it to be made public; but a kind consideration for her youth and inexperience, rather than any other feelings, she thinks, must have been the moving cause in your Grace's favourable notice of it. The remaining volume would have been printed long before this; but the last twenty-two weeks have been devoted entirely to her mother, who is not yet able to walk. I trust it will now be printed with as little delay as possible; and I think it will prove to be much more interesting than the other.

My daughter, who is here called both Miss Platt and Miss Tattam, has entered into my studies from her early childhood, and is of the greatest use and comfort to me in my parish, and the Sunday School; and in taking charge, with her mother, of my Clothing and Sunday School Benefit Societies, and in keeping up an intercourse with the female children, and influence over them after they have left the school. She will second, I am sure, as far as she is able, any efforts of mine to benefit the poor Copts.

I have the honour to remain, &c.,
HENRY TATTAM.

The Archbishop has indorsed this letter with the note, addressed, no doubt, to the Bishop of London, whom he expected to meet on his London day in the following week:—" Pray be so good as to look at this letter before we meet on Tuesday next. "W. C."

REV. H. TATTAM to the ARCHBISHOP.
BEDFORD, January 26, 1842.

MY LORD,

I trust your Grace will kindly condescend to pardon the liberty I am again presuming to take in addressing another letter to you in reference to the Coptic Church.

If I had no other evidence than Mr. Grimshawe's testimony, I should be led to doubt whether the Coptic Patriarch does sincerely desire the education of the Coptic priesthood through the instrumentality of the English. But from what Mr. Lieder has stated, who knows the Oriental character, I am induced to believe that he and the Copts do; and I think his cautious letter to your Grace was written under the influence of fear of the Egyptian Government, which I know constantly prevails among the Christian population.

I have not heard from Mr. Lieder since I was in town. . . .

I have no doubt that much wisdom will be required in dealing with the Copts, and that the spirit of kindness and gentleness and love must be in constant exercise. . . . It appears to me that error is best overturned by the establishment of truth. I would by no means conceal my opinions on the points on which we differ in faith and practice, nor would I needlessly bring them forward; but whenever called upon by persons or circumstances to do so, I would do so in the spirit of kindness, and in the language of Scripture. . . .

It appears to me, but I may be in error, that, in communicating religious knowledge to the Copts, it can only be effectually done through the medium of Scripture. I would venture respectfully to suggest, that a portion of Scripture should be regularly read and explained in the classes, either morning or evening, or at least once a day, until the whole of the New Testament has been gone through; and I should make Scripture as much as possible its own interpreter. The pupils should be permitted to ask questions after each lecture, and the next morning be required to bring as much of the lecture as possible in writing; which, after being examined and corrected, should be put by to be delivered to the writer when he leaves the school. In this way they would acquire a valuable stock of theological knowledge for future use, and a facility of committing their ideas to paper. In the course of the lectures the errors of the Coptic Church would come under review, and be shown to be unscriptural, without being directly opposed, and, if judiciously done, without, I should hope, stirring up the bad feelings of the people.

I am induced to hope that the Church Missionary Society will not think of establishing a school for those designed for the Coptic priesthood independent of the Coptic Patriarch: if they do, I fear they will be disappointed. The suspicions of the Copts, whom circumstances have rendered suspicious, would be excited, and they would keep aloof. They would imagine there was some concealed motive which would afterwards appear, as in the case of the Roman Catholics, who, as the Patriarch informed me, artfully introduced themselves among his people, and concealed their real sentiments until they had withdrawn a part of the wealthiest of them.

As the Patriarch has written to your Grace, I trust (in the absence of all information) that the Committee will request your Grace to agree upon a plan of education with the Patriarch. But if the Copts should decline to accede to such a plan as your Grace shall propose, it would, I think, be useless to attempt to establish a school without the concurrence of the Patriarch.

If your Grace should undertake this preliminary arrangement with the Patriarch, which seems to me the proper mode of proceeding, and it should appear to your Grace that by going to Cairo, and acting under your Grace's instructions, I could remove any obstacles, and facilitate the adoption of your plans by the Patriarch, I would willingly undertake the journey. I should then endeavour to obtain the remaining Syriac MSS., and see what I could further do in assisting to raise that fallen Church.

I have the honour to remain, &c.
HENRY TATTAM.

REV. H. TATTAM *to the* ARCHBISHOP.

BEDFORD, March 3, 1842.

MY LORD,

I have received a pressing letter from Mr. Lieder, intreating me to do all I can to obtain, at least, the New Testament in Coptic and Arabic, for the use of the Copts. I have therefore written to the Christian Knowledge Society on the subject; but before the letter goes, I have presumed to inclose it to your Grace; and if your Grace will condescend to do me the favour to peruse it, and, if it contains any thing objectionable, to return it to me again, I shall feel very deeply obliged to you. I will not trouble your Grace to write to me, but only to strike your pen through anything objectionable in the letter. But if your Grace sees nothing to object to in it, perhaps your Grace will further do me the favour to permit your Secretary to seal it, and post it. And may He who has the hearts of all men in his hand favourably incline the Committee to the request.

I have the honour to remain, &c.
HENRY TATTAM.

To the SECRETARIES *of the* CHURCH MISSIONARY SOCIETY.

41, BLACKMAN STREET, BOROUGH,
May 18, 1842.

GENTLEMEN,

I presented for your inspection some time ago a rough sketch of the desired plan, in answer to your request, for the consideration of the Committee, in regard to the "remodelling the Society's seminary at Cairo, so as to give a superior education to the youths educated therein, and that with a special regard to the Coptic Church;" and, as you in general approved of its contents, you desired me to draw up a correct copy for the inspection of the Committee. Since that time I have had an interview, especially in regard to it, with the Rev. Henry Tattam, at Bedford, who resided for a considerable time at our Mission establishment at Cairo; whose mature and sound views are well known, and who is not only practically acquainted with our proceedings there, but especially with the spiritual work of the Coptic Church. He entered with me minutely into every point of the proposed plan, to which he gave his full approbation; but as I received from him, after my return to London, an important letter in which he not only in general expressed his full concurrence with my own views, but gave some essential hints for the improvement of the plan, I considered it my bounden duty to embody some of them into the matter already given, especially those which affect the number of pupils, the teachers, and the financial department.

Preliminary Rules and Propositions for this intended Institution.

§ 1. As this Institution is situated in the heart of the Coptic quarter, which belongs to the outskirts of Cairo, and in the immediate vicinity of the Coptic patriarchate, it is my firm persuasion that it ought, as a trial, for at least the space of three years, to the end of 1845, to be opened, not only with "a special regard" but *exclusively* for "the benefit of the Coptic Church;" and that, if there should be found one or two subjects amongst the pupils of the present seminary who do not belong to the Coptic Church, and who should show not only considerable talent, but *especially* give hope that their hearts and lives are more or less influenced by the renovating power of the Spirit, that they ought only to be received and kept as exceptions, in regard to the rules of the said institution.

I feel myself the more obliged to press this point, as so many hopes have been offered to the Copts, in regard to the willingness of the Church of England to give them the necessary help, and especially the proposition to open for them an institution for the education of a superior priesthood for their Church, which by them was accepted (above expectation), and negatived by the Committee of the Church Missionary Society; and that only after a proper trial of the above-mentioned proposition (to open the institution at first exclusively for the Copts), when it should appear that it does not meet the expected favourable support from their side, then to throw it again open to all, Mohammedans as well as Jews, and Christians of all denominations, yet consisting *only* of day scholars; and in that case it would be profitable to transfer the said institution into a more central position for the diffusion of general instruction, namely, between the quarters of the Copts, Greeks, and Mohammedans.

§ 2. That this institution *ought to consist only of boarders*, as a Missionary Society can only undergo the expenses for keeping pupils as boarders in one of their institutions *with an especial view to promote individual conversion*, as far as it depends from human means; and to have therefore these favoured subjects under the immediate eye of the Principal of the institution, not only to have their minds constantly influenced and surrounded, as it were, by a Gospel spirit, but to preserve them particularly from the bane of the demoralising usages by which they might be infected from without.

If, on the contrary, these boarders have daily intercourse with day scholars, who come to receive their lessons with them, the hopes of the Committee in regard to these boarders will be *constantly crippled and defeated* (according to my own experience). An institution of this kind ought, therefore, either to consist entirely of boarders or day scholars; and, this taken as a rule allowance should only be made, on either side, for scarce and extraordinary exceptions.

§ 3. *The fixed number* of pupils in this institution during the first three years *should not be less than twelve;* yet ought the principal to be authorised to raise (during the course of the above-mentioned period) the number of its inmates to *fifteen*. The object of this proposition is important; it is to enable the principal to receive a pupil into the institution, if one or the other well qualified youth should desire to enter the said establishment.

The pupils ought to be chosen with great circumspection from those who are within the present seminary and boys' day school; then from those who may from time to time offer themselves from without these establishments. Its principal should carefully avoid all haste in filling up this fixed number of pupils; to which he may feel himself the more tempted, as he is in want of the same number of assistant teachers for six as for twelve and even twenty-four pupils. And as it is not easy to exclude a received pupil from the institution, not only from probable but even real causes, every pupil who enters the institution ought to know that his first six months' stay in it is only probationary, and that he may be liable to be sent away either during that time or at the end of it.

§ 4. That, though the pupils of this institution shall receive a *general and liberal education,* yet I believe that the plan of it should be drawn up and the lectures given with a *constant* intention to render them *all, what for the future may make them fit for preaching the Gospel,* as well if chosen for the ministry in their own Church, as, if not, for general or specific Missionary purposes.

A youth brought up thus, should he not feel himself inclined or called for the ministry, but choose any other honourable branch of life, will always be the gainer for an education of this kind, as he will be able to express himself correctly, either by writing or by speaking; and if his heart is touched and enlightened by the truth as it is in Christ, he may become a blessing to those around him.

§ 5. As " the system of education " in this institution " shall be wholly under the direction of the Committee, and therefore entirely dependent on the control of members of the Church of England, I would propose that the principal, who may lead the devotional exercises of the institution (during the week or on the Sabbath) should introduce either on Sunday afternoon or in the evening the beautiful liturgy of our Evening Service; the more so, since the Common Prayer Book has been translated into the Arabic language. The hall of the institution ought to be open during that time, to all who are either led to it by curiosity or who wish to join in the service; and, to make this service the more acceptable to the Coptic and Arab Christians, there might be introduced chanting, *in so far* as it is used throughout the churches of London, and which is of so purely an Oriental character. I believe that our edifying, evangelical Church service will attract many people, and that it cannot otherwise than produce a beneficial effect upon their minds; the more so, if they compare it with the unevangelical and, in dead languages, deadening liturgies of their own Churches.

§ 6. That there ought to be held in that institution *an examination every six months*, which should be open to all who wish to attend it. An examination of this kind would prove, I believe, to be especially useful and instructive, if there would be invited for the occasion the higher dignitaries and priests of the Church, as also intelligent laymen.

§ 7. As an institution of this kind can only prosper (in as far as God Almighty deigns to do His work upon earth by human instrumentality) if the Missionary, as its principal, endeavours to gain the entire confidence of those who are put under his fatherly care, so as to become, as it were, the soul of the institution, he ought to be dispensed, if required, with other Missionary business; for to be able not only to do the work intrusted to him in a general sense, but to follow it up in all its ramifications.

§ 8. I would finally propose, that the principal of the said institution ought to be *personally responsible*, not for accidental or unforeseen consequences, but *for the faithful execution of the duties in the work intrusted to him;* in as far as the Committee, in full consideration, can expect it from the East, where a Missionary's work is often more or less interrupted by indisposition.

And that the Committee ought to expect, in regard to an institution of this kind, not only some general account in the Annual Report of the Mission, but *a special Report* from its principal *after every half year's* examination.

I would further recommend to the consideration of the Committee, in regard to these preliminary propositions, the §§ 2, 3, and 7 of Mr. Tattam's valuable letter.

I shall now express my views in respect to *what is to be taught in this institution, with observations regarding the system, according to which the different scholastic branches ought to be given to the pupils.*

1. *Languages:* the Arabic, Coptic, and English.

(*a*) *The Arabic.* In this language the pupils ought to receive instruction in reading, writing, orthography, grammar, and composition, especially on texts of Holy Writ, until they are able to compose a sermon according to the standard rules of the Church. Declamation of select beautiful portions of literature; and one evening of the week is to be fixed in which the pupils have to deliver from memory their compositions, as a preparatory means for future preaching of the Gospel, to which exercise strangers may be permitted to be present. The principal and the assistant teachers of the Institution ought of course to be present at such a time; not only to watch and raise the respectability of the exercise, but also to express at the end of it their opinion to the pupils, if they think it proper, as well on their compositions in general, as also an approval or the contrary, respecting the delivery.

(*b*) *The Coptic.* In this language the pupils ought to be instructed in reading, writing, and grammar, so far, that they clearly understand, and are able to translate, what they read. Though it is to be pitied, that this dead language must be introduced into this institution, yet it is unavoidably necessary; for, being the sacred language of the Coptic Church, the pupils could never enter the ministry of that Church without it. (See § 4 of Mr. Tattam's letter.)

(c) *The English.* I would recommend, as one of the greatest improvements, that the English language is to be fully introduced into this institution, so far, that it becomes to the pupils, next to their native tongue, a living language. In this language they have to receive instruction in reading, writing, orthography, grammar, and exercises in speaking; so that they not only become competent to speak, read, and write it correctly and to use our excellent literature, but to translate useful works from the English into their own language; for I believe, that we have to look not only for able, but what is most important, pious translators, from such an institution.

I would further remark on this head, that a number of such young men, who are fully able to translate any work, religious and scientific, will be, for Egypt and the Arab countries in general, of the greatest importance, as well in a *religious* as (what is not to be overlooked) in a *moral, civil,* and *political* sense; *for it was chiefly from want of such men, that until now that bane of French literature, and by it French ideas have been introduced into Egypt, that so mighty an influence has been attained by that power, and* BY IT POPERY.

2. *Arithmetic.* This branch of education, I believe, ought to be taught in Egypt not according to our system, but according to that used by the Copts; for of what use is ours to the pupils, if those who have to investigate their calculations do not understand the way by which they came to the results? And besides this, the Copts have always been famous as accountants, and possess, as far as I have been able to ascertain, in their system peculiar facilities, so that it even may be possible, that our own system might be improved by that in use among them.

3. *Singing theoretically,* and especially of a liturgical kind.

The advantages derived from this branch of education are so well known and acknowledged, that I shall not enlarge upon it.

4. *Rudiments of Geometry,* as a useful branch of education, by which the pupils are taught and accustomed to think and to reflect.

5. *General Geography* and *the use of the Globes,* to which may be added an outline on *the Physiology of Mankind.* As a peculiar, interesting, and highly requisite part of geography, the lecturer ought to enlarge on *the geography of the Holy Scriptures.*

6. *Rudiments of Astronomy,* especially of a practical nature, which ought to be given in such a way, as to be a worthy comment on the nineteenth Psalm.

7. *The History of the Old and New Testament.* Along with these sacred historical lectures proper regard ought to be paid to *Chronology;* and to make that branch the more useful to the Coptic pupil, the chronology of the Hebrew and Septuagint sacred text of the Old Testament ought to be given in parallels, and their respective worth considered ; as not only the Copts, but most of the Oriental Churches have adopted that of the Septuagint.

I would further recommend, that the lecturer ought, in an introduction to Bible History, to enlarge on the *authenticity* of the sacred text in general, and of the special books which form it in particular.

8. To this branch of education most naturally follows *Church History*; which, properly speaking, is only a continuation of the history of the New Testament, and whose epoch is only finished, when "the kingdoms of this world are become the kingdom of our Lord, and of his Christ" (Rev. xi. 15).

9. *Bible Doctrine,* or what is usually called *Body of Divinity,* *with continual references to the Evidences of Christianity.*

The lecturer on this important branch of education ought

carefully to avoid *all* party peculiarities, and give the doctrines as revealed to us and warranted in the word of God.

The lectures on Bible Doctrine ought, if possible, to go along with the lectures on Bible History, as being so entirely dependent on each other as the woof is to the warp.

10. *Critical Explanation of some portions or books of the Sacred Text*, based upon *grammatical, historical rules;* so as to give the pupils a clear view, how the Holy Scriptures ought and can alone be explained without falling into error. Finally:

11. *General History*, with continual reference *to Bible History*, or the Theocracy as found in Bible History; from which alone its dark and crowded pages can receive light, meaning, and importance, and without which it would only be an unprofitable story book.

REMARK.

In regard to all the above mentioned historical branches, I would recommend, that the lecturer should divide every branch into two different courses; for, as it is evident that they not only are the most interesting part of instruction, but most calculated to form the mind of the pupil, the way in which they are taught *is far from being indifferent.* The first course of every branch ought to be carefully divided into short, clear, and systematically arranged epochs, according to the most prominent events, which form focal and turning points in history, and by which the memory of the pupil is powerfully assisted according to ancient and sacred experience: "The words of the wise are as goads, and as nails fastened by the masters of assemblies which are given from one shepherd" (Eccl. xii. 11). And only then, when he finds that his pupils are perfectly at home in those prominent epochs, he has to enlarge upon them in a second course, entering into details more minutely from the large store of that historical branch he teaches.

In concluding this part, I would observe, that the above noticed eleven scholastic branches I consider sufficient, if carried out, not only to enable those who have received a competent knowledge of them to become intelligent and useful members of human society in general, but that they comprise all that will for the future enable them, by Divine grace, to become the "ministers of Christ, and stewards of the mysteries of God" (1 Cor. iv. 1).

I am fully aware of the importance of the original languages of the sacred text; yet considering the present state of the Eastern Churches and what they require, I believe that the study of these languages would not be profitable at the present time; for they would occupy so much time that the pupil would have, on account of them, to neglect more general important branches of his study; and, after all, we must allow, upon historical, indisputable ground, that a man may be, by the grace of God, a distinguished instrument in the ministry and in the Lord's vineyard in general without the knowledge of Greek and Hebrew. At the same time I would say that, if an individual in this institution should show not only heartfelt piety, but at the same time uncommon talent and inclination for study, that he, as an exception, should be allowed by the Church Missionary Society to come to England to receive instruction not only in the Oriental languages of the sacred text, but in other branches which may be deemed necessary, and which at present cannot be given in Egypt from want of time and teachers.

I have now to answer the question—*By whom shall be given in the Institution the above-mentioned scholastic branches?*

§ 1. It is my firm persuasion that not only in this proposed institution, *but in any Missionary institution* whose principal has not yet the aid of able and converted native assistant teachers, that the important branches mentioned under Nos. 7, 8, 9, and 10, namely, Bible and Church History, Bible Doctrine and Critical Explanation of some portions or books of the Holy Scriptures, must unavoidably be given by the principal himself; if ever instruments fit as labourers for the harvest of the Lord shall reasonably be expected from such an institution. He would also have to take a considerable share in the lectures of geography; namely, in that special branch of the geography of the Holy Scriptures, as also in those of general history, for to throw *light, life*, and *meaning* into that important branch of education. A further immediate duty of the principal ought to be *carefully* to direct and watch over the compositions of the pupils on texts of Holy Writ.

§ 2. *The English language*, carried out to the extent recommended in (*c*) No. 1, can *only be given by an Englishman*. He should be an efficient person, destined for the Missionary work, who may acquire the knowledge of the Arabic language and the necessary experience while he is labouring in the institution; and who, by degrees, may become able to carry on the duties in case of sickness, or absence, or death.

An experienced and pious English master, who especially is endowed with sound views and heartfelt humility, would be, beyond doubt, a special blessing to such an institution.

Besides the English language, he would have to give lessons in the branches Nos. 4, 5, 6, and 11, namely, Rudiments of Geometry and Astronomy, Geography, and General History; for these branches must (on account of the present state of education in Egypt) be unavoidably given by an European teacher.

But his duty would not only be to teach the above-mentioned branches of education, but *to be the immediate assistant and confidant of the principal*, especially in watching with him over the moral and religious state and progress of every inmate of the institution—to go out with them when they take an airing, to be about them in the house as much as possible, and, if he should be an unmarried man, either to sleep in the same room with the pupils, or at least as near as the location will allow.

But I would add that, as the principal has to make himself personally responsible for the proceedings of the institution, this assistant ought to be under his control, to insure *unity in the execution of the different duties which such an institution demands*. (See § *b* of Mr. Tattam's letter.)

§ 3. No. 2, Arithmetic, and the Coptic language mentioned in *b*, No. 1, ought to be given by a Coptic teacher, and I believe that these branches might be given with much ability by Abuna Tekla; having been, before he was made a priest, an accountant in the service of the Government; and who is now also the best Coptic scholar in Cairo. Since about eighteen months he is employed to teach the Coptic language in the boys' day school, and would be glad to have this additional engagement.

§ 4. No. 3, namely, theoretical singing, might be given by Mr. Metri; as also the following other branches in the Arabic language, namely, Reading, Writing, Orthography, and the first introductory course of the Arab Grammar; for the second course would be necessary a Mahommedan Scheick, as there is in Egypt not a Christian to be found who is able to lecture in this difficult branch of that language.

Having expressed my views in regard to the persons who are necessary, besides the principal, for to teach the proposed scholastic branches in it, I shall finally try to settle *the important question: How much such an institution, according to the above given plan, would annually cost the Church Missionary Society?*

ANNUAL EXPENSES.

House-rent and Repairs	£60
Salary of the English Master and Assistant of the Principal	100
Salary of the Teacher mentioned in § 3, namely, Abuna Tekla	36
Salary of the Teacher mentioned in § 4, M. Metri	42
Boarding, Clothing, Kitchen-utensils, for fifteen Pupils and Servants	180
School materials, as Books, Slates, Paper, Pens, Ink, &c., &c.	12
Total	£430

If you compare the expenses of the present seminary during the years 1838–40, and consider not only the superior instructions which the pupils in the proposed institution have to receive, for to answer the design for which they shall be educated, as also the expenses of boarding and clothing, and that its inmates will be of riper years, and will therefore cost more, you will find *that the average mentioned sums are moderate.*

Should further details be required respecting this part of the plan, I shall be prepared to give them in a separate paper.

The salary of its principal I have not put down; because as a missionary he will have many other duties to attend to besides those in the institution.

I have also not mentioned the expenses for the first arrangement of the institution, as it regards the school and bedrooms; for I suppose that the sum expended for these purposes will be covered by the deficiency in the number of its inmates during the first year.

In concluding I shall only add, that I hope and pray, that our Committee will be able to grant this additional boon to the

Coptic Church; a Church which gives, fallen as it is, yet great hope (on account of its high veneration of the Holy Scriptures), that it may again be revived, by the grace of God, to its former importance, and as such become a Gospel-Pharos to the nations, not only to those in the immediate vicinity of Egypt, but also to those in Abyssinia and the interior of Africa.

Yours most faithfully,
JOHN RUDOLPHUS THEOPHILUS LIEDER.

COPY OF MR. TATTAM'S LETTER.

BEDFORD, *April* 18, 1842.

MY DEAR SIR,

§ 1. Although we have gone over your very important document together, in reference to the future seminary for the education of the Coptic priesthood, and have very fully discussed each head, yet I am sure you will forgive me, if I again advert to one or two points by letter. But before I do this, I beg again to reiterate, that I most fully concur with you in opinion in every part of your plan; and trust, under the blessing of God, that it will be an important instrument in diffusing Scriptural principles and real piety among the population of Egypt and Abyssinia.

§ 2. It is of the first consequence for the success of your plan, that you should secure the approbation of the dignitaries of the Coptic Church and of the chief persons among the laity to it. I would therefore suggest that a copy of it should be presented to the Patriarch at the earliest period, and the fullest explanation given to every part of it, and their approbation be secured to the plan before it be carried into effect.

§ 3. It appears also desirable that full admission to the institution, at all times, should be given to the leading members of the Coptic Church, to remove every feeling of suspicion and distrust from their minds.

§ 4. I fully agree with you that the Coptic, as well as the Arabic, language must be taught in your seminary; *it being a regulation of the Coptic Church, that no one shall be ordained a priest, until he can read and understand the Coptic language.* Either this law must be rescinded, which is not very likely to be done, or you must enable the pupils to comply with it. But independent of this, the Coptic language will always be of the first importance to that Church, *as it is the language of their own authorised and ancient version of the Scriptures,* which we have every reason to believe will be the only standard to which they will appeal in their inquiries after truth.

§ 5. Another point is, I hope the Committee will extend *the limit of the number of pupils to fifteen* instead of to twelve, for the reasons we have considered.

§ 6. I would most earnestly beg you to press upon the Committee the necessity of having an efficient person for second, or English master; one able to carry on the duties in case of sickness, or absence, or death. It should be one destined for the missionary work, and who will be acquiring the Arabic language and other requisites while he is labouring in the institution. Indeed I see no reason why those missionaries who will have to learn the Arabic language should not finish their preparatory education at Cairo.

§ 7. I also think your plan should be submitted to the Archbishop of Canterbury as soon as it is adopted by the Committee.

Pray excuse this. I write in haste to be in time for the post.

I remain, My dear Sir,

Yours very truly,

HENRY TATTAM.

Rev. H. Tattam *to the* Archbishop.

BEDFORD, *July* 22, 1842.

My Lord,

It appears probable that I shall go out to Egypt about the middle of next month, either from funds furnished by the British Museum, or from those offered from another quarter. I therefore take the liberty of writing to your Grace respectfully to say that, if I can in any way be of service in the good cause of religion in Egypt, I shall be most thankful to be employed in any way your Grace may think proper; not in seeking to carry out my own views, but your Grace's wishes, to the utmost of my ability.

Mr. and Mrs. Lieder spent a few days with us in May; and he brought with him his plan for the regulation of the proposed institution for the education of the Coptic priesthood; and we devoted two mornings to the consideration of it. I particularly requested him, in a letter which I addressed to him on the subject of the regulations, to press upon the Committee the propriety of submitting the plans to your Grace at the earliest possible period, before they were finally adopted, for your Grace's suggestions or approval; and, as Mr. Lieder purposes to return at the latter end of this month, I would earnestly hope it has been done. I also took the liberty to suggest that the plans should be laid before the Coptic Patriarch, as soon as they conveniently could after their adoption, and that the fullest explanation should be given on every part; and that the Patriarch, the Bishops, and all the respectable Copts should have access to the institution whenever they may desire to do so; that they may have no lurking fears of any secret object beyond what is openly avowed.

I was very glad to learn from Mr. Lieder that the first letter the Patriarch wrote to your Grace was very different from the one your Grace received; he having been induced to write another by some of the people who were consulted on this subject.

When I go out to Egypt, if your Grace sees no objection to it, I should be glad to receive and be the bearer of a letter, either from the Bishop of London or yourself, saying that I am authorised to purchase any manuscripts that they may be disposed to part with, that we may think likely to promote the cause of religion; so that, as far as the Patriarch and others can aid me in the object, they will be helpers in that cause which we all wish to promote.

I had fully intended to go to Egypt alone; but Mrs. Tattam and my brother, knowing how ill I was while out before, are very anxious I should take my daughter: but I do not well see how this can be, unless the Trustees of the Museum grant me a certain sum, should they think proper, for my expenses; and I will pay the remainder out of my own pocket.

If I succeed quickly, I may be back in three or four months; but the probability is I shall be longer.

I have the honour to remain, &c.

HENRY TATTAM.

This letter is marked " A " [Answered] by the Archbishop.

SIR ROBERT PEEL *to the* ARCHBISHOP.

[Autograph letter.]

Private.

WHITEHALL, *July* 27 [1842].

MY DEAR LORD,

I write a line to state to your Grace that we shall be disposed to sanction the expenditure of the sum of £1000 on account of the proposed mission of Mr. Tattam.

The official Recommendation from the Trustees of the Museum

may be sent, and in the meantime the requisite steps taken, in order that Mr. Tattam may be enabled to prepare for his journey.

 I have the honour to be, my dear Lord,
Most faithfully yours,
ROBERT PEEL.

HIS GRACE THE ARCHBISHOP OF CANTERBURY.

I have sent the papers to Mr. Forshall.[1]

REV. H. TATTAM to the ARCHBISHOP.

BEDFORD, July 30, 1842.

MY LORD,

 I have had the honour to receive two letters from your Grace, which I beg respectfully to acknowledge. The one received yesterday brings the pleasing intelligence of one thousand pounds being granted for obtaining the Syriac manuscripts. This I trust will be amply sufficient, if not more than sufficient, for the purpose. I shall cut down my own expenses as low as possible; but I shall spare nothing to secure the manuscripts, if I find I am beset with difficulties, which may prove to be the case.

 I placed £200 in the hands of Mr. Krusé in the spring, and gave him permission to draw on me to an unlimited amount, if he could secure all the Syriac MSS. for me; but he has not obtained a single copy. Should he procure any before I arrive, which I do not at all expect, I shall consider them the property of the British Museum, and shall send them there.

 I am in treaty with a gentleman to take my curacy, and I

---

[1] The Rev. Josiah Forshall, Secretary to the British Museum.

believe I shall secure his services, so as to be able to leave with comfort about the middle of August. Should any party, whom your Grace may know, be disposed to avail themselves of our company, and experience, to Egypt, we shall be most happy to have their company; but, while in Egypt, our time and attention must be confined exclusively to the objects for which I go out.

I intend to continue to edit the Coptic New Testament while I am out; if I can receive the proof-sheets through the government bag, which I hope I can do.

I shall endeavour to go through their Arabic version of the New Testament with the Patriarch, and Mr. Mazarra (?) the most learned Christian in Cairo; and, if any *gross* corruption is discovered, get the Patriarch to correct it by their own Coptic version, which is a close and faithful translation from the Greek.

If the report be true, that complete copies of the Coptic Old Testament have been discovered in Upper Egypt, I shall get copies made of the parts we want, and induce them, if possible, to permit me to have the originals.

I also intend that my daughter, if she goes, shall collate as many of the oldest copies of the Scriptures in Coptic as possible, in order to obtain all the important various readings we can collect.

The printer has promised that the second volume of the Journal shall be finished next week; so I hope to have the pleasure to beg your Grace to do me the honour to accept a copy before we leave. While my daughter feels highly gratified that it meets with your Grace's approbation, she feels it is of far too humble a nature to merit, in the least degree, your Grace's condescending notice.

I have the honour to remain, with the greatest respect, &c.,

HENRY TATTAM.

Rev. Dr. Tattam *to the* Archbishop.

BEDFORD, *August* 10, 1842.

My Lord,

I take the liberty to trouble your Grace with a letter to say, that, Mr. Forshall has acquiesced in my suggestion, that it would be well to present the Coptic Patriarch with copies of the Coptic works printed in this country; and he will procure the Coptic New Testament and the twelve Minor Prophets printed at Oxford, and the Egyptian Lexicon also printed there, for me to take with me.

I also take leave to state, that the first proof-sheet of the Coptic and Arabic New Testament will be corrected this week and ready to take with me; and a second by the beginning of the approaching month, if it can be sent out in the government bag. The Arabic is the version in use in Egypt, as well as the Coptic. Should your Grace wish to receive a corrected sheet, I will request the printer to send one. The Coptic type has been cut for the purpose.

I yesterday inquired at Mr. Lieder's late lodgings; but the person has heard nothing of him since he left at the beginning of July for Germany. In his last letter to me before he left for Germany, he said he was going to see his mother, and should return about the 20th of the month, and towards the end of it depart for Egypt. I therefore presume he is gone. I did not go to the Church Missionary House, and I have not been able to learn elsewhere what is the determination respecting the proposed institution; but I will ascertain as soon as I can the exact state of things . . .

Mr. Forshall wished me to see your Grace before I leave London, and, on his return from the palace, on Monday, informed me that your Grace would see me on Tuesday, at eleven o'clock;

I shall therefore have great pleasure in being at the Palace at the time appointed.

I pray God of his great goodness to prosper us in the objects for which we are going out . . .

I have the honour to remain, &c.,

HENRY TATTAM.

REV. DR. TATTAM to the ARCHBISHOP.

BEDFORD, *August* 13, 1842.

MY LORD,

I have this morning received the inclosed letter from Mr. Venn, one of the secretaries of the Church Missionary Society; and in reply to it have stated that I will call at the Church Mission House on Monday after my arrival in town.

I have also received a letter from Mr. Lieder, who informs me that they returned from Germany seven days ago, when they found their child seriously ill; that they leave for Egypt the 1st of September; that the Committee adopt the plan for the Institution, and will give him his general instructions on the 26th of this month.

I shall ask on Monday, to be favoured with a copy of the proposed regulations, that I may bring them with me to your Grace.

I have the honour to remain, &c.

HENRY TATTAM.

Rev. Henry Venn *to the* Rev. Dr. Tattam.

Church Missionary House,
August 12, 1842.
My dear Sir,

Mr. Lieder proposes to return to Egypt (D.V.) by the steamer which leaves on the 31st of this month. I am at this time engaged in preparing the instructions of the Committee respecting his future missionary labours; and I feel it to be most important that I should have some conversation with you on the subject. If you can possibly spare me half an hour during your transit through London, I will endeavour to meet you according to any appointment which you may make. I believe the Bedford coach passes under Highgate Archway. My house is situated immediately above it; so that, should you travel by that line of road, perhaps it might be most convenient to you to call at Highgate on your way to town.

I believe that you saw Mr. Lieder's paper and added a few remarks yourself. Mr. Lieder's plan will be the basis of the proposed institution; or rather the existing establishment will be modified according to that proposal.

I feel anxious, however, about the English master, which seems to me to be essential to Mr. Lieder's plan, and no steps have hitherto been taken to secure one.

Mr. Lieder's present address is No. 9, Redman's Row, Mile-End.

I am, dear Sir,
Very faithfully yours,
Henry Venn.

The Rev. Dr. H. Tattam.

REV. JOSIAH FORSHALL *to the* ARCHBISHOP.

BRITISH MUSEUM, *August* 13, 1842.

MY LORD,

In compliance with your Grace's instructions, I beg to transmit a copy of the paper to be given Mr. Tattam as a guide for his conduct in Egypt. A copy of this paper has been transmitted to the Foreign Office with a request that it may be communicated to H.M. Consul-General at Alexandria.

I have also applied to Lord Aberdeen for an official letter of recommendation, and that the Consul-General may be directed to indorse the necessary bills of exchange; all which has been promised.

I will wait upon your Grace on Tuesday morning at Lambeth to receive your Grace's commands.

May I remind your Grace that two or three lines to the Copt Patriarch, commending Mr. Tattam to his good offices, would be valuable. . . .

I have the honour to be,
With the greatest respect, &c.,

J. FORSHALL.

MEMORANDA REGARDING MR. TATTAM'S MISSION TO EGYPT, AUGUST 1842.

1. Mr. Tattam proceeds to Egypt with authority from the Trustees of the British Museum to negotiate for the purchase of the ancient MSS. in the convent of St. Suriani near the Natron Lakes.

2. Mr. Tattam's personal expenses are to be discharged by

the Trustees, a statement of which will be made to them on his return.

3. In order to provide for these expenses, the Secretary is authorised to advance Mr. Tattam two hundred pounds previously to his departure from London.

4. If the above-mentioned sum should prove insufficient, Mr. Tattam will be at liberty to draw upon the Secretary for one hundred pounds in addition, on account of these personal expenses, whenever it may be necessary.

5. The expenditure which the Government authorises for this Mission being one thousand pounds (the cost of conveying the MSS. to England and other incidental expenses being estimated as one hundred pounds), there will remain disposable the sum of six hundred pounds. Though Mr. Tattam is of opinion that the whole collection of the convent may be acquired for a sum considerably less, he will hold himself authorised to go to the extent of six hundred pounds, if the collection cannot be obtained for less.

6. In fixing this limit, it is presumed that the number of MSS. remaining in the convent amounts to something more than two hundred; that they are chiefly written on vellum; and that in antiquity, preservation, size, and general character they are similar to the forty-three purchased from Mr. Tattam last year. Any difference in this respect may modify the terms of purchase; so that, if the collection should prove more numerous than is anticipated, a proportionately greater expenditure may be incurred. The average size of the volumes brought last year may be estimated at two hundred large 4to. leaves. The relative value of MSS. on papyrus, vellum, and paper may be taken as 4, 2, and 1. If Mr. Tattam should find any volumes or fragments on papyrus, these will require the greatest care in packing.

7. Mr. Tattam suggests that, in case of his succeeding in negotiating the purchase, he may probably be able to induce

the Superior of the convent to accompany him to Alexandria, and to receive payment in the presence of the Consul-General. This arrangement seems entirely satisfactory; but if there should be a difficulty in accomplishing it, Mr. Tattam will use his own judgment; and the Consul-General will be requested to indorse any bills which Mr. Tattam may draw upon the Secretary of the Museum before the 31st January next, so that the total amount does not exceed seven hundred pounds.

8. The MSS. which may be purchased will be placed by Mr. Tattam in the charge of the Consul-General, who will have them safely packed by his own agent, and shipped by the packet or other first-class vessel for England.

9. The agent will address the packages—" Secretary of British Museum, care of Messrs. Francis and Co., 9½, Tokenhouse Yard, London;" advising the Secretary of their shipment and the particulars of their contents, in order that an insurance may be effected in London against sea risque.

10. If Mr. Tattam should meet with MSS. in any of the neighbouring convents or elsewhere in his journey in the East, he is authorised to secure these also for the Museum in cases where they can be had at a reasonable price; so that the total amount of his expenditure for such MSS. does not exceed three hundred and fifty pounds, for which sum he may draw bills upon the Secretary. In cases where it is impossible to purchase the MSS., or even where they may appear of little or no value, a brief description of them will be useful and interesting to the MS. department.

11. All bills are to be drawn upon the Secretary at thirty days' sight.

12. Mr. Tattam will be so good as to keep a daily account of his expenditure, and to annex a direction, that, in case of his separation from his papers, these last may be sealed up by those into whose hands they may fall, and forwarded to the British Consul-General at Alexandria.

13. Mr. Tattam will also have the goodness to write from time to time, as he has opportunity; communicating, for the information of the Trustees, the progress he has made towards the fulfilment of his mission.

(Signed)   J. FORSHALL,
Secretary.

LAMBETH PALACE, *August* 16, 1842.

WILLIAM LORD ARCHBISHOP OF CANTERBURY, *Primate of all England and Metropolitan,* to HIS HOLINESS THE PATRIARCH OF CAIRO, *greeting in the Lord.*

MOST REVEREND PRELATE,

Whereas our well-beloved Presbyter, the Reverend Henry Tattam, a man of eminent piety and learned in Holy Scriptures, is going out to Egypt, under the sanction of the British Government, for the purpose of obtaining manuscripts, and collecting such information as may be of use in promoting the interests of our holy religion, I gladly avail myself of this opportunity of assuring you of the high respect and good-will which are felt by me, and the other rulers of our Church, towards your Holiness and the Churches under your care, and of our desire to render you all the assistance in our power. In proof of this desire on our part, Mr. Tattam will exhibit to your Holiness a specimen of the New Testament in the Coptic and Arabic languages, which is now in preparation for the use of your Churches; and he will be happy to receive any suggestions from your Holiness which may render the work more perfect.

I further beg leave most earnestly to commend Mr. Tattam to your Holiness' kind consideration, assuring you that any attention which may tend to facilitate the attainment of the objects of his mission will be gratefully acknowledged by me, and by the members of our Church, who unite with me in zeal for the advancement of the Christian religion, and in sentiments of high respect and regard for your Holiness' person and the Church over which you preside.

From your Holiness' brother in Christ,
W. CANTUAR.

Written with my own hand.

Within a few days of writing this letter, before the end of the week, the Archbishop was seized with an attack of Asiatic cholera which brought him to the gates of the grave. He had been receiving guests that week at Addington, amongst whom was the Bishop-designate of Gibraltar (Dr. Tomlinson); who was one of the five Colonial Bishops that were to be consecrated in Westminster Abbey on the Thursday following (St. Bartholomew's Day). The Archbishop's merciful and marvellous recovery from that illness called forth, as will be seen, a letter from the Coptic Patriarch, of congratulation on his recovery and inquiry after his health.

REV. J. R. T. LIEDER to the ARCHBISHOP.

CAIRO, February 10, 1843.

MAY IT PLEASE YOUR GRACE,

I have the honour to inclose a letter of congratulation from his Holiness the Coptic Patriarch, in which he thanks God for your merciful restoration to health. In translating this epistle, I have endeavoured to keep as close as possible to the Arabic text; fearing that, should I deviate from its peculiar Oriental character, it might lose much of its interest and effect.

Your Grace will hear with pleasure that a friendly communication has lately been opened between the Patriarch of the Copts and the Lord Bishop of Jerusalem.

Doctor Tattam told me, when in London, that he had presented for your Grace's inspection and approbation the plan for the proposed Coptic Institution, and that your Grace was fully prepared to answer the former letter of the Patriarch, of which I was the bearer. Knowing this, I took the liberty of calling at Lambeth Palace, just before leaving England; anxious to be your Grace's messenger to the Head of the Coptic Church, when to my sorrow I was told of your Grace's extreme indisposition. Should your Grace deign to reply to those epistles of the Coptic Patriarch, any letter will reach me through the means of the Church Mission House.

The news of your Grace's full restoration to strength and usefulness has given us all matter of deep thanks in Egypt. May God Almighty by His gracious Providence watch, guard, and prolong your valuable life for the benefit of the Church Militant at this important universal crisis, is the prayer of

Your Grace's

Most Dutiful and Obedient Servant,

JOHN RUDOLPH THEOPHILUS LIEDER,
Presbyter of the United Church of England and Ireland.

In the name of God the Benevolent, the Merciful.

In God is our Salvation.

The peace of our Lord, and our God, and our Saviour and Author of our life, Jesus Christ, who descended upon the assembly of the holy disciples in the noble and majestic hall of Sion, and filled their hearts with mysteries and lights, and gave them power to forgive sins, transgressions and crimes—May the same Divine peace, and its abundant safety, be bestowed, in spiritual and apostolic love and charity, to the personage of our amiable and beloved Brother, his Grace the Archbishop of Canterbury, Primate of all England. May the Lord our God establish him on his seat many years, and peaceful times in a lengthened life, and put quickly his enemies under his feet. Amen.

After abundant spiritual salutation, and exuberant affection to him, may the grace of our Lord Christ remain upon him. And if you deign to ask about our lowliness—many thanks to God—we are in good health and strength, through the blessing of your prayers and supplications and the assistance of our Lord.

Before all things, we wish to inquire after your perfect health —if it pleases God Almighty, we hope that you are in praise-worthy conditions. May now the good news not be concealed from your eminent and pure Holiness, that we received your letter in the most blessed time and excellent hour, by our reverend, venerable, and highly esteemed son, Mr. Tattam; and, having read and understood its contents, we praised God Almighty on account of the welfare of your Holiness.

We have received by the above-mentioned the part of the Gospel printed in the Coptic and Arabic languages; and may it be known to your Holiness that we have corrected it for him.

We were afterwards informed that you were suffering from sickness; and, as our Lord has restored you to health, we are exceedingly glad and joyful, that the personage of your Holiness is now enjoying health and peace. And with regard to our venerable son, Mr. Tattam, may he be perfectly quiet [at ease] in reference to what he desired of us.

May our Lord continue the love between ourselves and between you, by sending (us) all your news regularly for the ease of our mind in regard of you. May you enjoy a lengthened life, and its continuation.

The 1st day of the month Muharram, the year of 1259.

(*February* 1, 1843.)

ARCHDEACON TATTAM [1] *to the* ARCHBISHOP.

BEDFORD, *January* 4, 1846.

MY LORD,

Your Grace very kindly condescended to say that you would write a few lines to the Coptic Patriarch of Alexandria with the present of Macarius' Homilies.

There are one thousand copies of the Homilies in Arabic for the use of the Egyptian Christians; three hundred of which were sent off on the 8th of December and are now on their way to Egypt; and the others shall follow whenever the Patriarch may want them.

I have consigned them to the care of Alexander Todd, Esq., of Alexandria, and shall write in a day or two to request him to forward them to the Patriarch. The usual style of addressing the Patriarch is, His Holiness the Lord Patriarch of Alexandria. The letter should be addressed to him at Cairo, where he always resides.

If I have been the means of obtaining from them manuscripts that are perfectly useless to them, I rejoice that I have also been the means of presenting them with the Homilies of their own Macarius, in their own native language; and I believe the first portion of the New Testament in Coptic and Arabic will be ready to follow in less than a month. I expect to be in London one day this week, and will then do myself the pleasure to forward your Grace a copy of the Homilies. The copies for Egypt have no preface nor dedication.

Your Grace had the great kindness to offer a subscription towards the printing of the Homilies in a former letter, which I then respectfully declined; as Mr. Grimshawe and some of his friends had engaged to pay the expense of the printing, and I had already paid for the translation and copying of the manuscripts. Mr. Watts' estimate for the whole was £124 15s.,

[1] Dr. Tattam was appointed to the archdeaconry of Bedford, March 12, 1845.

and I told Mr. Grimshawe that £135 would cover all the expenses; but on Saturday morning I received Mr. Watts' bill, amounting to £163 15s. 4d. I shall therefore pay the £28 additional before I present the bill to Mr. Grimshawe; and if your Grace will have the kindness to favour me with any small donation towards it, I will thankfully accept it.

I should not have presumed to apply to your Grace under any circumstances, had you not kindly condescended to offer assistance.

I have the honour to remain, &c.,

HENRY TATTAM.

ARCHDEACON TATTAM to the ARCHBISHOP.

BEDFORD, *January* [5, 1846].

MY LORD,

I wished to have informed your Grace in my letter of last night, of the arrangements I have made with the Coptic Patriarch relative to the Coptic and Arabic versions of the New Testament we are now printing, but interruptions until post time prevented my doing so.

The constant variations of the Arabic part of the Coptic and Arabic manuscripts have caused both difficulty and delay, so that we have only now printed the Gospel of St. Matthew. Therefore, to avoid all perplexity and delay in sending the proof-sheets to Cairo, I requested a copy of all the Arabic editions of the New Testament to be submitted to the Patriarch, for him to make choice of one which Abouna Tecla should alter the text of, wherever it did not correspond with the Coptic version. The Patriarch fully approved of the plan proposed, and has made choice of the Arabic New Testament published by the Christian Knowledge Society in 1727, which is esteemed above all others in the East. The Abouna has returned me St. Mark and St. Luke's Gospels, altered here and there; and the other books will speedily follow, so that we shall go on printing from the present time without further delay. If I do not like any alteration of the Arabic text, as we proceed, I will submit it to Mr. Cureton; and if he agrees with me, we will restore the text of the *printed* copy. I have also sent over my Coptic New Testament, for the Abouna to collate with the Patriarch's best manuscript. He has returned me St. Mark and St. Luke with a very few variations in the margin, which I shall adopt or not, as the Greek readings authorise.

I wish also to state to your Grace that I have revised the manuscripts of St. Macarius, which I caused to be translated into good Arabic under the Patriarch's eye. The Homilies I had calculated upon being able to print through the aid of private friends; but we are compelled to rebuild my church, which is in a very dilapidated state; and from the great poverty of my parish I am necessitated to solicit contributions from my friends and the public for this object. I should be thankful if your Grace knew of any Society, the funds of which could be applied to the printing of the Homilies.

I have also got St. Chrysostom's Commentary on St. John's Gospel in Arabic, beautifully copied from the Patriarch's copy, which I should be glad to print; but I am sorry to learn that the funds of the Christian Knowledge Society cannot be applied to that purpose.

I have had two pages of St. Macarius set up, which I venture to send to your Grace;[1] the smallest type would cost about £120 for a thousand copies. I do not know what the cost of the larger type would be.

I have the honour to remain, &c.,
HENRY TATTAM.

[1] [Specimens of a page of each type were inclosed. The letter is marked "A," Answered.]

Archdeacon Tattam *to the* Archbishop.

Bedford, *Oct.* 7, 1846.

My Lord,

I take the liberty to trouble your Grace with a letter, respectfully to say that the edition of Macarius's Homilies in Arabic, which I partly promised the Coptic Patriarch, has been finished about a month, and is now in the hands of the bookbinder.

I think I stated to your Grace that when I was last in Egypt I was inquiring of the Patriarch if they had any of the works of Macarius in Coptic? to which he replied, with expressions of deep regret, that they had not a line in any language. This induced me to ask him if the Homilies were translated into Arabic, would they be acceptable to him and his people? To this he replied that we could not present him "with a greater boon, next to the Scriptures, than the works of our own Macarius." I therefore set a competent person in Cairo to translate them under the Patriarch's inspection; and they were afterwards submitted to a revision by Mr. Faris, of Malta; and the edition is now printed, and I hope will be ready to be sent off to the Patriarch by the beginning of next month, or at least a considerable portion of them.

I beg with the greatest respect to submit to your Grace, whether it is not desirable that the volumes should go as an offering, or rather present, from the English Church Association; if so, whether your Grace would condescend to write to His Holiness to announce it, and that they will be sent as speedily as possible, with our good wishes and prayers for the spiritual prosperity of the Coptic Church.

Trusting your Grace will kindly pardon this intrusion,

I have the honour to remain, &c.,

Henry Tattam.

Archdeacon Tattam *to the* Archbishop.

Bedford, *October* 17, 1846.

My Lord,

I have been honoured with your Grace's reply to my former letter this morning; and I beg further to state, for your Grace's information, that the edition of Macarius's Homilies consists of a thousand copies; that I myself paid for the translation into Arabic, and for the revision of the work by Mr. Faris of Malta; and that Mr. Grimshawe guaranteed the payment of the printing, by himself and some friends, so I trust there will be no difficulty on that head.

Since I took the liberty of writing to your Grace I have stopped the process of binding the work, at Mr. Grimshawe's suggestion, who wishes for a short preface in English to be added to twenty-five copies for distribution in England, stating the circumstances which led to the publication of the work. This I sent to the printer last night.

He also wished for a dedication, in Arabic, to the Patriarch of Alexandria, to be inserted, if possible, in all the copies. This I also posted last night with the other, a translation of which is on the next page. I find the greater part of the volumes are bound.

I have the honour to remain, &c.,

Henry Tattam.

Archdeacon Tattam *to the* Archbishop.

Bedford, *October* 31, 1846.

My Lord,

I am exceedingly concerned at having caused your Grace to write two letters; but I am very thankful that your Grace has kindly and condescendingly written the last, which I did not contemplate when I wrote. . . .

As I have not received a proof impression of the dedication from the printer, I shall stop his proceeding with it; first, because the greater part of the volumes are already bound, and, secondly, because it accords best with my own feelings and ideas. I am not aware that dedications are known in the East, and I do not want to parade my own name. My first idea I think was the best—that it should go without any addition, with a few lines from your Grace to the Coptic Patriarch, as your Grace has kindly consented to write.

I feel very much concerned at having caused your Grace to write a second letter; but I am very thankful that your kindness prompted you to do so, as your Grace has preserved me from falling into error.

I have the honour to be, &c.,

HENRY TATTAM.

SIR HENRY ELLIS *to the* ARCHBISHOP.

BRITISH MUSEUM, *October* 29, 1847.

MY LORD,

I have the pleasure to acquaint your Grace that Mr. Trevelyan, on behalf of the Chancellor of the Exchequer, has authorised me to announce to Mr. Pacho, that the Treasury close with his offer of £3,500 for the Syriac manuscripts from the monastery in the desert of Nitria, the remainder of the library obtained in 1841 and 1843 by Dr. Tattam.

I am, with much respect,

MY LORD,

Your Grace's faithful Servant,

HENRY ELLIS.

The month of November (1847) saw the Archbishop declining greatly in strength. He had heard, November 6, of the death of his aged brother, the Archbishop of York, the day before, without any previous intelligence of his illness; and the diary in which he was accustomed to note down the letters he had written each day, presented, in its almost entire blank, the signs of his inability to do more than what seemed pressing duty each day, and which he did not neglect. On the 20th of January he could not leave his bed, and on the 11th of February (1848), the day which was to complete the eighty-second year of his life, he was taken to his rest, in the thirty-fifth year of his Episcopate, and the twentieth year of his Primacy.

With regard to the institution, on the establishment of which so much care and thought had been spent, it must, briefly, be noted that, in 1847, Mr. Lieder's report, given for the year preceding, as contained in the *Missionary Register* for July, 1847, states that, amidst "much to discourage," there was "much more to cheer," and to "evidence that our great object, the elevation, through God's grace, of the Coptic Church," was "proceeding with much success; for the fullest confidence," he says, "is now manifested toward us by all the higher orders of the native clergy, without whose countenance all our labours would prove in vain. The Patriarch shows the kindest feeling towards the institution, and frequently gives his benediction to the pupils; while the amiable Bishop of Esneh, Amba Michael, is an almost daily visitor, inspecting and encouraging the young men in the pursuit of their studies. Amba Michael is often in Cairo on duty connected with the patriarchate. During his last visit he brought with him his sister's son, a fine lad of thirteen years of age, and, placing my hand on his head, told me to regard the boy as my own son; that, as he had dedicated him to the priesthood, he now submitted the whole of his theological studies to me."

In a later letter, however, dated February 11, 1848, Mr. Lieder expressed "the opinion that the institution, as it" was, was "not worth the great expense to which the Society was subject;" and the Committee at home, after considering Mr. Lieder's special report, corresponding "in its general tenor, with the above opinion," came "to the decision that the institution should be either abandoned, or carried on upon a greatly modified plan" (*Missionary Register* for June, 1848, p. 270). It was closed accordingly.

THE END.

www.ingramcontent.com/pod-product-compliance
Lightning Source LLC
Chambersburg PA
CBHW031119160426
43192CB00008B/1045